Praise for End the Silence:

The story of a girl whose childhood has been ripped in shreds and who is able to triumph over all the obstacles is incredibly compelling. The power of the human spirit is a universal theme: this book has the makings of a best seller.
Bianca Dias-Halpert, Founding Partner of The Indo Project

End the Silence opens a window to a little known chapter on the Pacific war of the 1940s. In a highly readable and thoroughly engrossing book, the authors tell the story through an eye witness account of a family caught up in the conflict and the birth pangs of the Indonesian republic that followed. It deserves to rank among the best of that period.
Dr. Orval Hansen, former member of Congress

Rage, shame, cruelty, hardship and compassion are deeply embedded in Ilse's story. This book becomes one of countless guardians of memories, one that dares to put an "end to silence." I recommend it highly.
Dr. Jan A. Krancher, The Defining Years of the Dutch East Indies, 1942-1949, Survivors' Accounts of Japanese Invasion and Enslavementof Europeans and the Revolution That Created Free Indonesia.

History comes alive and engages students when it is presented from the perspective of someone who has lived it. Ilse's story is both heartbreaking and uplifting. Students won't want to put down *End the Silence* until they have turned the last page.
John Kenneth Hansen, Professor, International Baccalaureate Schools

End the Silence

By Dorothy Read
and **Ilse Evelijn Veere Smit**

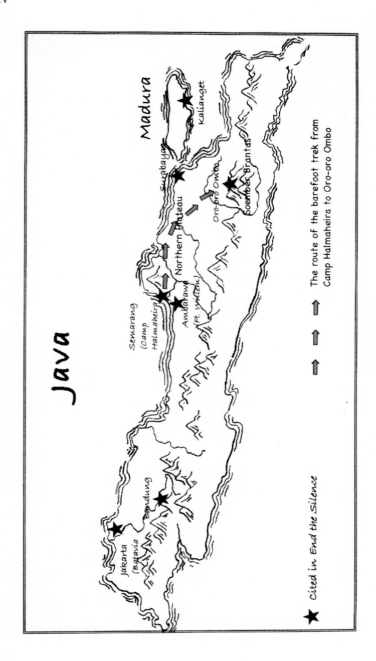

Java

Madura

Semarang

Jakarta
(Batavia)

Bandung

Surabaya

Kalianget

Camp Halmaheira

Northern Plateau

Ambarawa
(Ft. Willem)

Soember Brantas

Oro-oro Ombo

⬆ ⬆ ⬆ The route of the barefoot trek from
Camp Halmaheira to Oro-oro Ombo

★ Cited in *End the Silence*

v

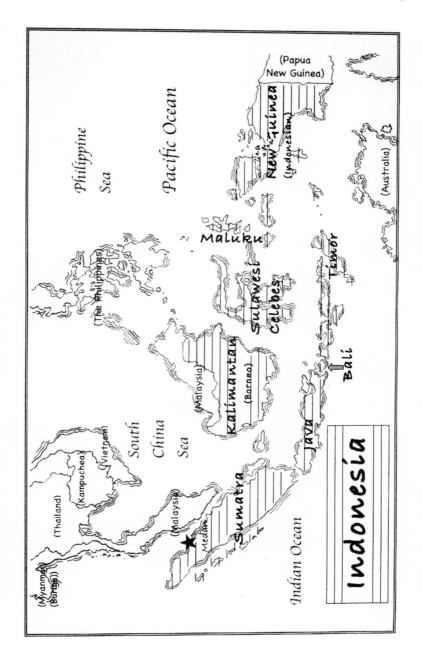

Double-Isle Publishing
Greenbank, Washington

ISBN: 1461181216
ISBN-13: 9781461181217
LCCN: 2011907868

Cover art: Pierr Morgan,
www.pierrmorgan.com

Authors' photographs: Michael Stadler
Stadler Studio Photography
www.stadlerstudio.com

I dedicate this book to my mother, Maria Evelijn Veere and to my husband, Jan Smit.

In loving memory,
Ilse Evelijn Veere Smit

TABLE OF CONTENTS

Author's Foreword

It is Thanksgiving Eve, and Ilse Evelijn Veere Smit stands at the pulpit explaining why she is thankful for the white handkerchief displayed in a picture frame beside her. She tells a tale of life and death in a Japanese concentration camp on the island of Java during World War II, when it was still part of the Dutch East Indies. Two hundred parishioners sit spellbound, myself among them. Many weep, shaken by the story of our friend—dainty, tea-colored Ilse, who speaks with a Dutch accent and sings in the choir.

As I listened to Ilse's story of the handkerchief that night, my heart connected with the little girl across the Pacific whose world collapsed and who discovered "anything that crawls, you can eat." Knowing she wanted to put her story into print as a legacy for her children and grandchildren, I offered to help. Thus began a remarkable relationship and hundreds of hours of conversation between two women who recall World War II in very different ways.

I had so much to learn, beginning with the fact that the Dutch East Indies in the old geography books became Indonesia after World War II. "Don't call me Indonesian," she says. "I am Eurasian." She inherited her Dutch citizenship and status from her European grandfathers, but she inherited her smooth, tawny skin and deep brown eyes from her island ancestors.

I learned, too, that the story goes beyond Ilse and her family; it deserves a world audience. It also goes beyond WWII, morphing into the Bersiap Period of Indonesian history when the native freedom fighters were determined to rid their island nation of all things Dutch. It is one of hundreds of thousands of stories of the Dutch and Indos caught in the chaes of the Indonesian revolution. The final chapters of Ilse's story deal with her attempts to cope with the trauma of those years in a family that refused to talk about it.

End the Silence is told from old memory. Although old memory carries historical treasures, it is sometimes at odds with modern practice. For example, the setting of this story is called the Dutch East Indies (DEI) because "Indonesia" and "Indonesians" came later. Old memory insists that the language of the DEI was Maleis, not Malay or Bahasa Indonesia. Old memory also insists that the people of mixed ancestry were known as Indies (Indiesa if they were women), not Indos. And finally, old memory recalls words as they were said, not as they were spelled, so we have done our phonetic best.

Old memory in no way implies faded memory. The events in this book come to us from the heart, the mind and the soul, through every physical sense. I am the conduit between these vivid scenes and the printed page. She lived it; I have recorded it in narrative form, supplying dialogue and details to support the stark reality of what happened. Although the events presented here are well documented, this is not meant to be textbook history; it is Ilse Evelijn Veere Smit's history, written as she remembers it.

D.R.

Whidbey Island July, 2011

End the Silence

Prologue

I am telling the story I needed to tell my father. True, it happened decades ago, but it is still present in my mind. It still seizes me with paralyzing fear. Ask my husband—I wish you could, may his soul rest in peace—about the times he had to coax me forward to the present after I was transported, by a sight or a sound, back to a concentration camp in Central Java. Or back to a tiny bamboo cell in a guerilla outpost in East Java. We didn't have a word for it then. Now they call it post-traumatic stress disorder and people go into therapy for it.

I was ten years old when I assumed the responsibility, alongside my gentle mother, of taking care of the little ones. My sister, Marijke, was only six, my brother, René, was four, and little Edith, a babe in arms when we entered the hellhole called Camp Halmaheira. Where was my father? We didn't know. The Japanese cleaved our family as neatly and as suddenly as a farmer separates a chicken's head from its body. I stepped into his shoes and did everything I could to keep his children alive, during and after Halmaheira. But my father never knew.

All my life I have been told I must put the past behind me, but the memories are still vivid. If I could have told my story, I might have put the awful images to rest. But that didn't happen. So I will tell it now.

The story must start before World War II, before the Japanese took over the Dutch East Indies, before the itching and the hunger, before the terror, before my island homeland became known as Indonesia.

Chapter 1.
Before the War

Our home was called the Dutch East Indies when I was born in 1933. We also called it the Emerald Girdle: more than 17,000 islands, a jewel of an archipelago adorning 3,000 miles of the equator. Nowhere on earth were the grasses greener, the bougainvillea more crimson—or cobalt—or violet. Nowhere else did the magnificent *waringins*—those banyan trees of my childhood—spread farther, nor the flamboya trees blossom redder.

The natives of the Dutch East Indies were called Javanese, Sumatrans, Balinese, Madurans, and so on, named for the island where they were born. The Dutch were Hollanders, wherever they lived. My family was Indies—mixed-blood, part Dutch and part islander—which, in my view of our colonial society, made us as Dutch as the blondest most blue-eyed Hollander.

Rebellion against Dutch rule festered beneath the surface of the Emerald Girdle, but not in my world. I had never heard of "Indonesia" or "Indonesians." Life was good for a little mixed-blood girl, an Indies *Miesje* growing up in the Dutch East Indies before World War II.

My father, Hendrik Evelijn Veere, was an educator with a university degree from Amsterdam. When he finished his schooling, the Netherlands government commissioned him to return to his birth land to establish Dutch schools. He was an important man, and I was proud of his standing in the community.

My parents always had horses, and they rode after the *middag dutje*, the nap we all took to escape the worst heat of the tropical day. The ride was the best part of my father's day, and he tried very hard to include me in it. But my horse phobia always took over. My father did not believe in phobias—a sign of weakness, he said, and he did not permit his children to be weak.

By 1938, when we lived in Medan on the island of Sumatra, I had learned some tricks for getting my own way. Every afternoon my father called me to the stable. Every afternoon he and my mother were on their horses by the time I answered the call. Every afternoon I stood my ground, in the shade of the fragrant plumeria trees that lined the stable path, and refused to get on the horse. Even then my father and I clashed wills.

"No, Papi, I do not want to get on the horse with you." I cross my arms and scowl my meanest scowl.

"I will not tolerate this, Ilse," says Papi. "You must get up on this saddle at once." His teeth are clenched tight, turning his mouth into a straight line without lips. He nods to the stable boy, our *katjung*.

As the katjung puts his hands under my armpits to lift me to my father, I raise my arms and sink to the ground. It is an old trick. The katjung takes in a long breath, blows it out, and bends to pick me up. I scoot backward, like a crab. The tiny gravel stones dig into my hands, but I am ready to scoot farther if I need to. I look back and forth between Papi and Mami. She looks very tall, as her back is so straight and her black hair is piled high on her head to keep her neck cool in the afternoon heat. Her head is turned just enough to see me. Her jaw is also clenched, but it is the type of clench that keeps a smile from breaking loose.

Now Papi says the dreaded words. "Ilse, if you do not ride with your mother and me today, I will send you to spend the entire afternoon with the *kokki.*"

"Oh, no, Papi!" I make tears come.

"Katjung, see to it," my father orders and he rides off with my mother.

As soon as they disappear around the bend in the lane, I jump up, smile at the katjung, and run off to the kitchen to join the *kokki*—our cook—who is my favorite person in the world, next to my mother. "My *babu kokki*" I call her, using the "*babu*" part which shows respect and means "female."

I pass the enormous steel sink which stands outside, against the back wall of the kitchen. This is where the food is sorted and washed. I stop to check for snails clinging to the sides of the sink and see only a few, not very big. No snail treats for the servants tonight. I would not dare to tell Papi that I have sampled them, but they are really quite good, the way Babu Kokki prepares them with spices.

I skip down the hall to my favorite place in the world.

The kitchen walls are white stucco, and the floors are big terra cotta tiles that match the fat little terra cotta cook stoves, the *anglos,* lined up against one wall on a long concrete bench. Bunches of red and green chili peppers are drying on black iron arms that swing out over the row of anglos.

The chopping and the slicing are done at low wooden tables. The best table, the one that smells of sweet and savory flavors, holds the *ulekans,* round flat grinding stones the size of dinner plates, and gourd-shaped mashing stones. Babu Kokki spends hours at the ulekans, grinding the spices—cardamom, nutmeg, cinnamon, coriander—too many to name. I am often set to smashing the coriander or the nutmeg, but never the hot red peppers that would bring on a choking fit if I should taste their seeds or smell them on my fingers. I stop to feel the handle of the smooth stone that was chosen from the river bed to fit my hand exactly. "*Anak* Ilse," Babu Kokki says, using the polite title "child" in addressing me. She speaks Dutch, but it is difficult for her. "Will you please bring me the *santen* from the ice chest?"

"What is it for, Babu Kokki?" I ask in Dutch. I see fresh grated coconut piled on the table we use for mixing delicious things. I am hopeful.

"Little Miss Curious," she laughs. Then she slips into *Pasar Maleis*, the peasant tongue that we are not supposed to speak in our home because Papi does not allow it. "Does it matter what it is for, or is it enough that your babu kokki asks you to bring it?"

I know I have been scolded. I deliver the bowl of coconut milk and stand beside her, head down, inspecting my bare toes for a moment to show I am sorry. Then I lift my head to watch her every move. She puts sugar into the great wooden mixing bowl and reaches for the eggs, cracking them one by one into the sugar. When they are mixed, she adds fresh churned butter and beats it all into a soft cream with her wooden spoon. She dumps in the coconut milk and then the sweet rice flour.

Then she says, "Before we can put in the shredded coconut, you will have to mix this batter until it is perfectly smooth." Her eyes open very wide, making them round like her face. "If you want *buah klappa quadrat,* that is."

I clap my hands for joy—sweet coconut pudding squares, my favorite dessert! I run for my *dinkliek,* the small stool I sit on to do work at the table. Babu Kokki takes the moment to smooth her *kondah,* the bun of wound-up grey hair that she fastens, with dozens of crinkled wire hairpins, to the back of her head just above her neck. I have tried to wind my hair up just so, but my kondah never stays put.

I stir with all my might as Babu Kokki puts charcoal into the belly of each of the anglos and fires up the little stoves. I can feel the soreness in my left arm, so I switch the wooden spoon to my right hand, my clumsy hand. At last, Babu Kokki comes to check the batter.

"Ah, you are a stirring genius, Anak Ilse. It is perfect. Now let's put in the coconut. Stir gently," she warns. "Make sure the coconut gets to every part of the batter."

I am so careful to spread the coconut evenly, and the buah klappa quadrat is finally ready to be poured into an oblong dish, covered, and put on top of one of the anglos. Babu Kokki piles a few hot coals on top of the cover of the dish, and the pudding is left on its own to bake.

Then Babu Kokki starts the cooking of the side dishes that will be served with the rice for dinner. I stay out of her way as she scoots from one anglo to another on her own three-legged dinkliek, tossing the meats and vegetables and sauces into the pans that wait for them over the hot coals. It is a dinkliek dance, from one to another of the six stoves. I begin to smell the coconut pudding, and I am very happy indeed.

Chapter 2.
The Doll House

By the time I turned eight, the world had begun to unravel in all directions. Japan was reaching out to pull the Dutch East Indies into its clutches, and the Dutch government had slid out of Germany's grasp by moving to London. But this grim news affected my life not one bit. We were back in Bandung, Java, my birth city and the perfect place to live, in my young opinion. On May 6, 1941, life in Bandung was still normal. I remember this because it was the best birthday I'd ever had.

I open my eyes to sunshine. This is my birthday! I jump out of bed. Oma and Opa Fiedeldij will be here this morning, and Tante Zus and Oom Ruud Doyer. All my favorite people—Mami's parents and Mami's sister and her husband, poor Oom Ruud. Papi plays tricks on him all the time, except when Oom Bert Fiedeldij, Mami's brother, is here. Oom Bert is an important person in the Air Force and he flies his own plane. "A real **Fee**-duhl-day," everyone says, perhaps because he is like his father, my Opa Fiedeldij. I am sorry that Oom Bert is not coming today. I wonder what Papi has in store for Oom Ruud.

I must hurry to get ready. Mami has put out a nice dress for me to wear to the train station. She and I will go to pick up Oma and Opa soon after breakfast. Papi is busy doing something else—I don't know what, because it is a secret. Oh, I hope it has to do with my birthday present. Last year he made me a headboard with Mickey Mouse painted right in the middle of it. My Mickey has music coming out of his wide-open mouth. Papi figured out how to connect Mickey's mouth-speaker to the phonograph, so every night Mami asks me what I want to hear as I drift off to sleep—Brahms, Schubert, Strauss, Beethoven. I love them all, and I love my Mickey Mouse headboard. My sister, Marijke, has Donald Duck. Perhaps when he moves into a real bed, little René will have Goofy on his headboard.

I get to go with Mami because I am the birthday girl. It is great fun to meet the train. Oma Fiedeldij waves madly out the window so we know which car they are in, and then we run to greet them and get our hugs as they step off the train—from Oma, that is. Opa, being Dutch, is not inclined to show affection in public.

When Mami and I return with Oma and Opa, they shake hands with Papi who tells our *djongos*, the butler, to bring in the suitcases. I am anxious to get the hellos over with so we can get on with celebrating my birthday.

At last, Mami puts her arm around my shoulders. "Ilse," she says, " I want you to close your eyes."

"Why?" I ask, pretending to be suspicious.

"Because Papi has a surprise for you," she says. "Come, I will lead you."

To make the surprise even more fun for them, I act as if I don't trust them. My eyebrows are right down on top of my eyelids, I am frowning so hard. Mami and Papi laugh and

Marijke jumps up and down. She knows the secret, but she hasn't known it for long or she would have blabbed. Oma, holding little René, and Opa look as if they are anxious to see the surprise. They are always impressed with Papi's inventions.

I close my eyes and let Mami lead me away. I can tell we are going toward my bedroom, with Papi and the others right behind us. Marijke giggles nonstop. This must be a very good surprise.

"Open your eyes," Mami says.

I open my eyes, and I don't seem to be in my room at all. It takes a moment to figure out what I am looking at—a huge wooden wardrobe that takes up nearly a whole wall. It is divided into three sections, each with a decorated door that has a star in the middle made of different wood shapes and colors.

Papi steps over to the door on the left and opens it. My dresses are all hanging on a rod inside the cabinet, and on the inside of the door itself, a mirror taller than I am. I gasp, I am so surprised and so happy to see such a fine closet.

Papi steps over to the right side of the wardrobe. He opens the door to reveal shelves—some deep, some more like cubbyholes. My nightgowns and undies and play clothes that do not hang up are all folded and arranged on the shelves, and my shoes are in the cubbyholes. I see two drawers as well, for treasures I would not want to put on open shelves. It is exactly what I want, to keep my belongings neat and tidy, and I clap my hands.

"Ilse, your father made this for you," Mami says. "Wait until you see the rest."

The rest? I would be happy with only what I have seen so far.

"Close your eyes one more time," Papi says. This time I do not question. I just close my eyes up tight until he says, "Okay, open up."

I open my eyes onto the most beautiful doll house I have ever seen, built right into the middle of the wardrobe. A three-story house with stairways. I see a parlor, a dining room, a kitchen, bedrooms, an office, and even a water closet and a tiled *mandi bak* for bathing. Every room has doors that look like they will open and close, and tiny furniture. Wallpaper decorates the walls, and the tile floors have colorful woven rugs. Tables have lamps on them, and chandeliers hang from some of the ceilings. My mouth is wide open. It is so beautiful I cannot speak. Then Papi flips a switch inside one of the walls, and the lights go on inside the doll house.

I can't help it; I burst into tears. "Oh, Papi," I say, and run into his arms.

"Here, here, why the tears?" he says. "Don't you like it?"

"It is the most beautiful thing I have ever seen in all my life," I sob, and I mean every word. My Papi can make anything, and he can figure out how to do the cleverest things.

"Magnificent, Henk," Opa Fiedeldij says. "How long did it take you to build it?"

"Oh, long enough," Papi answers. He turns me around and gives me a little pat. We are through hugging and I am through crying.

"Ilse, may I play with it?" Marijke asks.

Marijke is only four, and I'm not sure she is old enough to be trusted with the tiny pieces in my doll house. I hold my breath and do not answer, but Mami comes to the rescue.

"No, my love. This is Ilse's doll house. You are too little to handle the tiny furniture."

"But when you are older, you will have one," Papi tells her. I do not think Marijke is satisfied with that. I will have to keep a close eye on my doll house.

René wants to get at the doll house, too, but the grown-ups know better than to let that happen. He is only two years old. They leave the room, taking René and Marijke with them so that I can investigate the doll house by myself. The doors do open and close. They are on tiny hinges. And a little carved toilet sits at the back of the water closet. I am sure no one in the world has ever had such a doll house. One by one, I pick up the delicate pieces of furniture and begin to arrange them to my liking.

When I hear Oom Ruud's car in the driveway, I run to greet my aunt and uncle. I can't wait to show my new present to Tante Zus. Everyone is hugging and handshaking and talking all at once, the way they do when Mami's family gets together. Finally I get Tante Zus's attention.

"Tante, you must come and see what Papi made for me." I am giggling just like Marijke, I am so excited to show off my present.

First, the dress closet. "See, Tante, I can look at all of myself in the mirror!" I am hoping she has brought a new birthday dress for me to hang in the closet. She is a wonderful seamstress, like my mother. Both of them have sewing projects going on all the time, and Mami even keeps a needle and thread tucked under her collar, just in case a button needs to be put back on or a hem needs to be repaired on short notice.

Then I show Tante Zus the shelves. I am saving the middle door for last. But just as I open the door to reveal the doll house, we hear the most terrible clatter from another part of the house—pop-pop-pop, like gunshots. We rush out of the room and follow the sounds to the cement hallway that leads to the water closet. Mami and my grandparents come from a different direction, and we all arrive just in time to see Oom Ruud run out of the bathroom door, yelling his head off. But he can't go very fast because his trousers are down around his ankles. Papi is leaning against the wall, laughing so hard he can hardly stand up.

"All right, Henk, what have you done this time?" Tante Zus says, holding her full skirt out on both sides to hide Oom Ruud as he pulls his trousers back up where they belong. She throws a look at Mami, as if she expects her sister to do something. But my mother just rolls her eyes upward and shrugs her shoulders. I think she is working hard not to laugh.

Papi is crying by now, with laughter, so he doesn't answer Tante Zus. Opa Fiedeldij walks into the water closet and comes out with a string of little black ladyfinger firecrackers in one hand and, in the other, the basket of silk flowers that decorates the back of the toilet. They are black, too.

"Okay, Henk, how did you rig this one up?" he asks. He doesn't seem to be very amused. I think Opa must be a real Fiedeldij, too.

∘◡◦

The rest of my birthday celebration was quiet by comparison. Of course my aunt would not speak to my father, as usual. He was half-Dutch, too, and a gentleman in anyone's society except when Oom Ruud came around. I'm quite certain he spent the interims between my uncle's visits inventing new practical jokes. I honestly can't imagine why Oom Ruud ever agreed to come to our house.

When it was time for my grandparents to go home, my grandmother balked at getting on the train. Bags packed, they went to the station and waited on the platform. When the train pulled in, my grandmother would not climb aboard. "We will go tomorrow," she said. The train she refused to board ended up at the bottom of a ravine. No survivors.

My grandparents went home the next day, and I never saw them again. I do not know what became of them. I do know that Oma Fiedeldij passed her gift of foresight on to her daughter, Maria Christina Fiedeldij Evelijn Veere—my mother, Mies.

Chapter 3.
War Comes to Bandung

Oom Bert showed up later in the summer of 1941 with disturbing news that Japan had begun to bomb our neighbors. We could be next, he said—Japan wanted our oil. I remember how everyone laughed when I suggested we just give the Japanese some oil, and then they wouldn't have to bomb us.

When Oom Bert left, my father built a bomb shelter in the back yard, well camouflaged by a raised flower bed. I wondered why it needed to be camouflaged, as if a Japanese bombardier would purposely aim a bomb at a family hiding under the ground. But I did not question the need to be under camellias and sunflowers and hibiscus.

Then, in December, Japan bombed Pearl Harbor, and our part of the world was at war.

Even with the threat of war hanging over our lives, my mother and father continued to work in the elementary school where she taught and he presided as headmaster. She had been university educated, too, in Amsterdam. Their education and Dutch fathers may have given us status, but status didn't protect us from Japanese bombs. For that, we had a humbling hole in the ground. The siren would begin to wail, warning us of Japanese planes on the move. I remember running to the shelter, installing my earplugs, and putting a thick piece of rubber, like a school eraser, between my teeth. Then just waiting and listening. Sometimes we actually heard airplanes passing overhead and my heart would pound in my ears and I could not let the breath out of my lungs. But no bombs fell on us, and war seemed distant.

That all changed in January 1942 in Bandung, Java, when I was still eight years old.

Mami is planning an art lesson for her class. She has run out of the special paper she needs for the project.

"Ilse, Marijke, comb your hair and change your clothes," she calls. "We need to go to Van Dorp's." Van Dorp's is a wonderful place—a big book store where we children can almost always find a book or a craft project to bring home. I prefer arts and crafts to books. I am like my Papi who paints pictures on wood, with oil paints.

Marijke and I just woke from our midday naps. We shed our nap-wrinkled coveralls for playing and put on dresses for going out, freshly laundered by our *babu tjutji*. In the tropics, where clothes are changed several times a day, the babu tjutji keeps very busy.

"Come, my darlings," Mami says, reaching out to put the finishing touches on Marijke's brown-black hair. Marijke is only four years old, and her hair is already so thick the comb sometimes gets stuck. My hair is not nearly as pretty, but I try not to be jealous. Mami checks to make sure we have our ear plugs and our rubber mouthpieces. They hang on a ribbon around our necks twenty-four hours a day. I put mine inside my clothes so they don't bob around when I'm playing sports.

I am quite good at athletics, especially at *discus werpeh*. When I wind up, around and around, I can sling the discus farther than anyone else in school. I cannot have pieces of rubber flying about my head at such a time, nor when I do the *farspringen*, the broadjump, which I usually win also.

It is a typical sun-washed tropical day, but not too hot, so we walk, Marijke and I beside our mother, and in the stroller, our brother, René. His little toddler legs could not make such a long walk. We walk under the overhanging flamboya trees that line the boulevard leading to the shopping area. The red blossoms are thick, a colorful canopy to protect us from the sun.

"Do we get *ice lilin?*" asks Marijke. We all love the red and green crushed-ice treats sold by the Javanese street vendors.

Mami laughs. "I don't think so, little one. I think your papi would find out, and we would have to listen to a lecture on the dangers of eating ice lilin. We do not want to upset him just now. But perhaps some good *kuweeh mangkok* would do instead."

"Yes, yes," we cry. Little René, too, loves the sweet, steamed muffin cakes and he claps his hands.

"But Mami, why can't we ever have ice lilin, when it is so delicious?" Marijke asks.

"Because it is made with river water," I answer. "And everyone knows river water is full of poopoo." Little sisters can be so annoying.

"Then why do you swim in the river when we go to meet your friends at the park?" Marijke asks. "If you know it is full of poopoo," she adds, as if that needed to be said.

The stroller stops. Mami looks at me while I avoid her eyes. "Ilse?" she asks.

"Mah-RAY-kuh, be quiet," I say, pronouncing each syllable to let her know she is in trouble with me. "And besides, we don't go to the park any more without Mami or Papi, since the airplanes have come." I hope I can change the subject. We are forbidden to swim in the Cikapundung River. My father says we can get terrible diseases from it—diseases that the native islanders do not get because they are used to the water.

"Ilse, your papi and I had better not catch you swimming in that river."

I am silent; I know the rule. But it is a silly rule since we always watch for the floating poopoo and warn each other to get out of the way. And as many times as I have sneaked down to swim in the Cikapundung, I have not once gotten sick from it. I do not talk to Marijke the rest of the way into town, to pay her back for tattling. I would like to pull her hair, but that will have to wait until Mami is not watching.

True to her promise, Mami takes us first to the *warong* which sells the best native treats NOT made with river water. It is a big wagon on the sidewalk, with many people around it as it is very popular. When it is our turn, we each select a plump cake, and we ask for chilled coconut *kolak* with little chunks of banana in it to refresh us after our long walk. It is my favorite drink. Then on to Van Dorp's.

We reach a six-way intersection where a policeman stands on a raised island in the middle of the traffic circle, directing cars, bicycles, horse-drawn carts, pedaled taxis, and pedestrians. We can see Van Dorp's across the circle. All of a sudden the sirens start. At first people run in all directions, shouting. The policeman jumps down from his platform and disappears into the crowd. Traffic stops and people jump out of their vehicles. Then everybody runs toward the bookstore with its huge windows and wide overhang, and we run with them. We are trying to hide under the overhang, out of sight of the airplanes which have machine guns as well as bombs.

All huddled together, the crowd becomes silent. Then, there it is, the sound of airplane engines far off, like droning bees. I am looking for them, specks in the distance. Suddenly my mother grabs Marijke and me by the hands, to pull us from the crowd. Pushing the stroller and herding us girls, she runs toward the street. From the overhang behind us, people are screaming at her to stay. They are cursing her, yelling that she is crazy and selfish.

"Why don't YOU just go?" "Leave the children here!" "Crazy pig!" they shout.

We are crying, terrified, running as fast as we can to keep up with Mami. "Faster, faster," she cries as we race across the traffic circle toward a street lined with trees on both sides.

We can hear the airplanes very well now. Oh, they are getting close. Pulling up under a broad flamboya tree, we are across the street from a house with a bomb shelter in the front yard. Strangers are calling us to come in. The bombers are in clear sight. We race the last few yards to the shelter. Arms reach up to lift my sister and me down the stairs to the floor of the shelter, and then René, stroller and all, with my mother right behind just as the heavy wooden door slams shut. Mami pulls René from the stroller and collapses on a bench. Marijke and I press close up against her, and she wraps her arms around the three of us. We gasp for breath as the ever-present earplugs and rubber mouth pieces are stuffed into place. Planes roar overhead; everybody prays.

And then—an enormous explosion. Dirt sifts down on us. The wooden walls of the shelter shake, as if there has been an earthquake. Then it becomes very, very, quiet. Eerie. No sounds of birds or barking dogs above us. No wind. Nothing. We wait until the sirens tell us we can leave the shelter.

"Thank you," my mother says over and over to the people who pulled us into their shelter. In the dim light of the underground room, I can see other children, one about my age. They all have blond hair. Hollanders. One, older than I, is helping a very old lady stand up. There are several Javanese servants. A blond-haired man climbs the stairs and swings the door open. Now we hear people screaming off in the distance.

Standing on the surface, beside the bright flowers which hide the bomb shelter, we look toward the traffic circle and Van Dorp's, beyond. Mami puts René into the stroller, never taking her eyes from the place where we had just been such a short time ago. We inch along, toward the smoking ruins that are between us and home. When we reach the intersection, I try not to look, but I cannot help myself. The horror. Where the policeman had stood is now a great big hole. The people hiding beneath the sidewalk overhang are now just one bloody mass. Millions of glass splinters, wood and metal mixed with flesh. Screaming. Groaning. Crying. We hear sirens, the kind on ambulances and fire engines. Help is on its way.

We turn away from Van Dorp's and walk fast, in silence, while I try to get the picture out of my mind of what I have just seen. I think I will never succeed.

Chapter 4.
De Hotel

We fought valiantly, I understand, with the help of the Dutch, British, Americans, and Australians. But on February 28, 1942, eight days after the Japanese marched into Bandung, the Netherlands gave up the Dutch East Indies. Most of our defenders were captured and ended up in forced labor gangs in Burma. Some—like Oom Bert, thank God—escaped to Australia. Some went into hiding to conduct subversive activities against the Japanese.

Oddly, I remember nothing of a shooting war going on around us. Perhaps that was because we had moved to Surabaya in East Java. Who knows why we moved during that period of fierce fighting? Surely the Dutch government did not transfer my father to a new school—schools would not have been a high priority between January and March of 1942. I suppose my father thought he was moving us to a safer place.

Our new home was much like our previous homes—a comfortable estate surrounded by the usual *brandgang*, an alleyway formed between us and our neighbors by high cement walls topped with glass shards. The brandgang served the dual purpose of keeping fires from spreading from one house to another as well as keeping thieves on the other side of the wall. Thievery was a problem on both sides of the wall, however, in a place where servants had so little and their employers had so much. My father solved that problem by hiring people from different islands who would not hesitate to snitch on each other. Babu Kokki, of course, moved with us and soon had the new staff under control.

And so, by February 28, 1942, we were settled comfortably on the other side of Java, waiting to see what would happen next. It didn't take them long to get to Surabaya.

My first view of the Japanese was not at all what I expected. They came into the city on bicycles, hundreds of bicycles. I don't remember much else about that first sighting, but I do remember their hats—little hats with bills in the front and long white flaps hanging down the back. No one on Java wore anything to protect their necks from the sun, and so we laughed, my sister and I, at the sight of the mighty Japanese pedaling along on their bicycles with their white pennants fluttering along behind them.

Once the Japanese had arrived, my father did not permit us to leave our estate. We watched the Japanese go back and forth in front of our house. Marijke and I always had to suppress our giggles over their ridiculous appearance. But we didn't laugh for long.

Marijke and I are in the glassed-in *voor gallerie* making flower dolls with hibiscus blossom skirts. Before we even realize what is happening, two Japanese soldiers walk right up the steps, past the pillars that hold up the roof, across the verandah, and through the door into the front room where we are sitting. It is like they think they live here. Marijke and I are dumfounded.

Mami must have seen them coming because she comes into the front room. "Henk! Henk!" she calls to my father.

The soldiers seem polite enough. They click their heels together and nod to my mother and then to my father. Papi asks them, in Maleis, what he can do for them.

I can barely understand their Maleis, but they repeat enough times and make hand gestures until I understand that we have to leave our home. We will have only one day to get ready, and we can only take what we can carry in suitcases.

"But where are we to go?" Papi asks, and one of the Japanese gives him a piece of paper.

"This will entitle you to rooms at De Hotel," he says two or three times, until he is sure Papi understands.

Mami looks like Job's wife, struck into a pillar of salt, rooted to the floor. But she manages to ask, "Why?"

"Others will need this house now," says the taller soldier, only once, but we all understand. Then they nod once more, snap their heels, spin about and march out of our house. We watch them pick up their bicycles at the gate and ride off.

Mami and Papi look at each other and Mami bursts into tears. Just then, René walks in with his little orange-striped kitten which is not supposed to be in the front room. Mami doesn't even notice. She is drying her tears with her handkerchief, the one I embroidered for her last birthday, her favorite one, she says.

Papi finally speaks. "Children, we are going to move."

Marijke and I already know that, but René is excited. "Do I get to take my kitty?" he asks.

"This move is different, son," Papi says and he pats René's shoulder. "We can take only what we can carry in our suitcases."

René hears "suitcase," and he runs out of the room, probably to fetch his teddy bear which always travels with him. Marijke and I go to Mami and Papi, and we all hold onto each other for a moment until René reappears. He is waving his little brown treasure, its button eyes hanging by thick threads and its nose matted from repeated soakings.

My little brother has taken care of his packing, but the rest of us have many decisions to make. Babu Kokki helps Mami pack and repack—clothing, linens, sewing supplies, dishes, cookware, toys, things we can carry to our new hotel home. The servants must stay behind. I wonder what it will be like to live in a hotel without my babu kokki.

De Hotel is big, with lots of wings. Hundreds of families already live here. Our apartment is at the back of the building. Four rooms: a bedroom for our parents, a bedroom for us children to share, a tiny living room and a kitchen. Small but okay, as far as I'm concerned. We can smell the aroma of many meals in the hallways—satay, peanut sauces, spicy condiments. Mami adds to the fragrant mix with the meals she prepares— not the many side dishes we got from our babu kokki's kitchen, but there is always rice with something delicious on the side. It is a good thing Mami taught cooking at school. Otherwise she would not know anything about it, as that would be the kokki's job.

The best thing about De Hotel, in my opinion, is that we don't have to go to school. The Japanese closed them. They also burned books—the ones written in Dutch and English. I am sorry about some of them—the ones I like—but Mami and Papi got very emotional, and Mami cried about it. It is forbidden to hold school of any kind, so every day is play day, and I have plenty of playmates at De Hotel.

One problem, though, is that without school we are without pencils and paper and art supplies. We could really use some chalk for both drawing pictures and for drawing out *hingke* squares on the sidewalk so we can play hopscotch. But we can get into trouble for having school supplies, so chalk is out, even if we knew where to get some. But I think I might be able to make the next best thing—*arrang*! And I know exactly how to do it because I have watched my babu kokki make charcoal a hundred times. Yes, with charcoal we can make drawings and hopscotch squares on the sidewalks and not get into trouble, unless I get caught stealing matches. I will have to be very careful on that, and on choosing a place for the fire. Behind the great waringin tree out in the corner of the front lawn would be ideal. The dirt should not be too hard to dig, and the tree will hide us from anyone that might come up the drive or walk out on the front verandah. Not that anyone will do either—no one ever uses the front entrance of De Hotel. It is forbidden.

Getting the matches is the easy part. I just get up in the middle of the night, tiptoe to Papi's jacket hanging over the back of his chair, reach in, and pull out a little box of them. I take a few out of the box and put the box back into the jacket. Oh, I am so quiet, and I hide the matches under my pillow.

At last I am on my way to the play yard, matches deep in my pocket. I choose two trusted friends to help me. We must find good branches, just the right size—not too small or they will burn too much. Not too big or we will not be able to break them off the trees, and also, they will not burn enough. And not too long, as we cannot dig a very big fire pit. I also have a spoon in my pocket, a big one that will remove the earth properly.

My friends are expert wood gatherers, and in no time at all, we have twelve perfect branches, each about two inches across and seven or eight inches long. We head for our secret burning place behind the waringin. I find a large patch of bare dirt between the roots that stretch out and cross over each other.

Dig, dig, dig. We take turns with the spoon, which is handy for chopping through the little pieces of root we find. If Mami misses the spoon, I will have some explaining to do. I will have some explaining to do anyway, if I can't get this poor spoon bent back the way it is supposed to be.

"Do you think the roots can catch fire underground?" says Pieter.

"Naw," I answer, as if I really know whether they can or not.

The hole grows to about a foot square and a foot deep. We gather up the tinder-dry leaves that have fallen on the ground and collected up against the brandgang wall. We put a nice thick bed of leaves across the bottom of the hole. Now we stack the wood: four side by side on the bottom, with space in between, four criss-crossed across the top of those, and the last four back across the middle row. We stuff leaves down the sides of the hole, and down between the stacked wood. Now, leaves across the top, and we are ready to light it. Oh no, I have nothing to strike the match against. Pieter runs off and returns with just the right rock for striking matches.

The first match goes out before it gets to the leaves. I moved too fast. I lean right over the leaves and strike a second match, but it also fizzles out before it ignites anything. Oh oh, only three more matches.

"Here, give me the matches," says Walter who is eleven and sometimes tries to be in charge. He strikes a match, cups his hand around it the way Papi does when he lights a cigarette, and he lights the leaves. Very professional, I think, and I wonder if he knows how to smoke. I might ask him later.

Now it is time to cover the fire with loose dirt. Not too much or the fire will go out, not enough and the fire will burn too fast and we will have ashes instead of charcoal. I take charge of this part, and I sprinkle dirt over the fire, quickly, just as I remember seeing Babu Kokki do it.

We watch until we have to go back in for lunch. When we leave, we can see smoke rising from underneath the dirt, but not enough to be seen by any adults, we hope. Oh, yes, we will have charcoal soon, for drawing and for playing hopscotch on the long, broad sidewalks in front of De Hotel. When we put out the fire, though, we will pour a lot of water in that hole. If those roots catch fire, it could put an end to our playground.

We have other things to occupy our time, besides sidewalk art and hopscotch. The hotel brandgang has huge, high concrete walls, and along the top the jagged glass shards are of different colors that sparkle. Very pretty. But it is also very mysterious. We are curious about the enormous wooden door with black iron hinges. It opens into the brandgang alleyway. We try to pick the lock every day, but it is useless. The door remains closed, and the longer it remains closed, the more we long to get through it.

And then, good news sweeps through the play yards.

"The door is open!"

We swarm to the place and slip through the opening into the forbidden space. I find myself in a narrow alley—perhaps as wide as our driveway at home, and dirty. It is a place for garbage and bad deeds. I am fascinated as I sift through the filth—a braided ribbon here, a deflated soccer ball there, all dirty but washable. And then I find the prize—a fat balloon with a wide top. I hold the slippery thing firmly between thumb and forefinger and run for home.

Down the long hall and through our door, I can hardly wait to wash my balloon and then blow it up. I have never seen a balloon quite like it. I am three steps inside the kitchen when my mother turns and sees me. "Aeeiiii!" she screeches, bringing my father to the kitchen.

"Drop it!" he shouts, and I do.

"Where did you get that thing?" he roars.

"It's a balloon, Papi, and when I wash it with soap and water—"

"Under the faucet," Mami orders and in no time she is lathering my hands.

"Where did you get that thing?" Papi asks again.

"In the brandgang," I whisper. Mami gives me an embroidered towel. Then she snatches it back and gives me an old scrub cloth to dry my hands.

"To your room!" Papi orders before he stomps out of the kitchen. I expect he is on his way to chase my friends out of the brandgang and put an end to the fun. "For the rest of the day," he adds as he disappears into the hallway.

In my room, I wonder if I am being punished for stealing or for going to a forbidden place. It is a lot of fuss over a strange-looking balloon.

❦

The charcoal experiment worked, and the months passed uneventfully but pleasantly for us at De Hotel. Probably our activities were curtailed, but for us children it did not feel like imprisonment. I am sure it was different for my parents.

Chapter 5.
Christmas, 1942

At the end of 1942, the adults must have known of the dire state of the world on two fronts, but none of it filtered down to us children. We were aware, only, that Christmas was approaching.

December 5th is a day of great anticipation for Dutch children, no matter where they are in the world. It is the Day of St. Nicholas, when St. Nick himself comes riding off a boat on a white stallion, accompanied by Black Peter and his men. St. Nicholas carries a gunny sack full of toys and treats. Black Peter carries a book with children's names and the yearly record of their deeds. Worthy children are rewarded with toys and goodies from St. Nick's bag. But it is a day fraught with anxiety, as Black Peter's men carry gunny sacks, chains, and brooms. They are looking for naughty children to chain up and then whisk into the empty gunny sacks to be toted off to Spain, never to be seen again. Of course little Dutch children, including those of mixed blood, try to influence the final judgment by leaving cookies in their shoes on St. Nick's Eve, along with carrots for St. Nick's horse. Children go to bed knowing that St. Nicholas will be slipping down their chimneys—or in the case of those living in the tropics, some other aperture—while they are sleeping. If they are lucky enough to wake up in their beds and not in a gunny sack in the bowels of a boat headed for

Spain, the children will find presents waiting for them in the living room.

St. Nicholas' Day was a skimpy affair at De Hotel in 1942. There would be no gifts and there was little heart for makeshift parties that would remind us of what we had lost and of our uncertain futures. But my parents made an announcement that wiped away our gloomy attitudes and brought us more joy than any gift from St. Nick's gunny sack.

I wish René would hurry up with his dinner. Mami has made a delicious coconut pudding to celebrate the Day of St. Nicholas, and I am anxious to get to it. I must be scowling because Papi leans close to me and scowls, too, but I know he is teasing. Papi does not tease very much these days.

"Ilse, you are not happy on this December 5th, eh?"

"I will be happy when Mami brings out the coconut pudding." I can't help but laugh. Papi looks so funny with his face all scrunched up.

Papi laughs, too, and reaches across the table to take Mami's hand.

"Your mother has something to tell you that will make you happy," he says.

Mami clears her throat, and we know it is something important. Maybe we are going back to our house. Or better yet, to Bandung. She pats her stomach.

"In a few months, my darlings, you will be getting a new little brother or sister."

Oh, how excited we are! Marijke and I talk about what we will do with our doll-baby sister. René chatters on about his new little brother. We eat our dessert. It is a good St. Nicholas' Day, after all.

It is April 22nd, 1943. I know because it is exactly two weeks before my tenth birthday. I have been marking the days on the calendar. Mami is not feeling well. She walks from room to room, and sometimes she stops to hold her breath and groan. She must be very sick. Marijke, René and I follow along behind her, not sure what to do.

"Mami, shall I go find Papi?" I ask, although I have no idea where he might be.

"No, darling. He will be back soon." She stops to groan again. "Why don't you take the children out to play?"

I would not feel right about leaving Mami right now, so I just take the little ones into our bedroom to play a game of hide the thimble. We have just begun when I hear Papi come in the door. We all run out to tell him Mami is not feeling well, and I almost run into a woman I have never seen before.

"Oops, child," she says to me. And then to my father, "Perhaps the children should go out to play for awhile."

"Of course," Papi says.

"Why?" I ask. I do not want to go outside while Mami is feeling poorly.

"Because I said so!" Papi is exasperated.

I don't know what to think. Who is this stranger, and why is Papi upset? And why are we being sent away?

Mami, as usual, knows just the right thing to say. "Henk, don't we have some sugar cane to send outside with them?"

Papi manages a smile and goes to the kitchen to get the treats. Mami groans again, this time a long, deep groan, and she reaches out to the lady who holds her steady. She puts her arm around my mother.

"I think it won't be long, Maria," the lady says, and suddenly I realize what this is all about.

Mami and the lady—I think they call her a midwife—disappear into the bedroom. Papi passes out the treats and shoos us out the door.

René is busy sucking on his stick of sugar, but Marijke is near tears. "What is wrong with Mami?" she whimpers.

"She is going to bring the new baby out," I tell her, hoping she doesn't ask for more details as I am not at all sure about how that happens.

We take a long time with our pieces of sugar cane, and we tell everyone in the play yard that we are getting a baby brother or sister soon, although it seems to be taking quite a long time.

When Papi finds us, he can't wait to tell us the news.

"You have a little sister," he says, and Marijke and I dance up and down. We gather up René and hurry back to the apartment.

Edith is so small and pretty. My heart makes little leaps inside my chest when I see her lying in Mami's arms, wrapped in a white cotton cloth. I already love her, and I can tell Marijke does, too. René stares at her and reaches out to touch her little face. He doesn't seem to mind she is not a little brother. Edith is all rubbed down with coconut oil. She smells delicious and her hair is shiny black. And curly!

I make a promise to myself that I will be a good big sister to this little one. And I decide that as a big sister of THREE young children, I will give up the childish habit of calling my parents Mami and Papi. From now on they will be Mam and Pap. I will start now.

"Oh, she is precious, Mam," I say and I stretch out "ma-a-a-m" a bit. It rhymes with "Tom."

Mam blinks at me a couple of times, and then she glances at my father. They both smile, first at each other and then at me. I feel I am much more grown up than I was earlier today.

From the vantage point of maturity, I can only imagine how Mam must have felt about bringing a new child into that world of uncertainty. But no one would have guessed she was anything but joyful over the birth of Edith. Pap—which rhymes with top—was equally joyful. Children were important in our family.

There was once another child, my brother Erik, four years older than I. He was only five years old when his appendix burst, and the doctor mistakenly treated it as stomach flu. I heard that when the little boy screamed in agony, my parents rushed him to the hospital, but it was too late. They said my father went crazy in his grief, and people had to hold him down to keep him from killing the doctor who misdiagnosed the problem. I don't doubt that my father loved us enough to kill for us, but I sometimes felt I had to earn his love. My mother's love was always at hand, however, and it was unconditional.

Chapter 6.
Satu Salah, Semuah Salah

While we had been looking forward to the arrival of our new baby, the Japanese had been supporting the eventual birth of another baby: an independent Indonesian republic. It was a symbiotic relationship. The nationalists would depend upon the Japanese to help them shed Dutch rule; the Japanese would depend upon the nationalists to help them strong-arm the Dutch in the East Indies. Sweet deal, if you were a Japanese or a nationalist. We were neither; we were Dutch. Our privilege, so taken for granted until now, worked against us. The Japanese claimed themselves to be the "Protectors of Asia."

We did not know how it would all play out. One thing we did know, however: the Japanese were conscripting able-bodied Dutch and mixed-blood Indies men to work in forced labor camps. We knew it was only a matter of time before they would come for my father, but we could not have guessed how that would happen.

I love to play pretend games, and De Hotel is one of the best places for that. The front entrance is my favorite spot. We are never, NEVER allowed to go up the stairs, however; it is absolutely forbidden, and we all abide by that rule.

But we can imagine. It can be a prince's *kraton*—a palace. It has white marble steps lined by rows of carved railings on each side—Pap told me they are called balusters. The wide handrail that runs along the top of the balusters is green marble, curved and cool to the touch. My friends and I can be barons and baronesses wandering about the palace lawns. I like to play the princess. The grass is a bit overgrown at the moment, but we overlook that as well as the weeds that have grown up in the rows of bright flowers along the walkway that leads from the curved driveway to the beautiful stairway. I suppose we could pull some of the weeds, but I would just as soon imagine them away.

The very best, though, is the sweet jasmine. It winds around the iron railings all across the front of the hotel verandah. The fragrance just floats through the air and I breathe it in as deep as it will go. Some parts of De Hotel have become shabby—I suppose because so many people are packed into it. But the jasmine makes up for it.

Today my friends and I are in the front yard under the waringin tree. The long roots hang down from the branches, reaching for a piece of earth to settle into. They make excellent swings. But this day the tree is our house The roots outline the rooms, and we are playing at being grown-ups. The real grown-ups don't bother us because they are not allowed to use the front entrance, either. We have the place to ourselves.

I am the kokki, preparing a pretend feast of crushed willow pods to serve in hibiscus bowls with our pretend rice in our pretend dining room.

"Now you must twist the ends, like this," I tell my *kandoki* whose job it is to assist me when she is not out doing the pretend grocery shopping, which is her main job. I show her how to get every little flake from the willow pod. She is a very good kandoki, even though she is only four years old.

"You are a genius," I tell her, and everybody laughs.

Then we hear the sound of an engine. This is strange. We all turn to see a truck speeding up the driveway to the front entrance. It is a Japanese army truck with a tan cover over the bed. It barely comes to a stop before Japanese soldiers start pouring out from under the tan cover. How can so many soldiers get into one truck? They carry rifles with bayonets stuck onto the ends, and they wear helmets, as if they are going into battle—not the silly caps with white flaps. They don't even notice we are here as they rush past us to the marble stairway. They take two stairs at a time and then they run, clomp, clomp, clomp across the verandah. We hear their boots clatter down the cement steps that lead to the hotel basement. The Japanese crash right through the door at the bottom of the stairway.

"What is happening?" we whisper to each other. Before anyone can think of an answer, more trucks come—empty ones. We all run to tell our parents what we have seen.

"Pap! Pap!" I yell the second I get through our doorway, and he comes out of the bedroom in a hurry, probably hearing the fear in my voice. But before I can get my breath, shouting fills the hallway. We hear doors being kicked in.

Our door is already open, and before we know what is happening, two soldiers walk in without a word and begin to tear our apartment to pieces, starting in my parents' room. I run as far from the soldiers as I can get—to the corner of the living room. On my way by, I pull the baby out of her drawer-bed on the table. Marijke and René jump up from their chairs at the table and follow me. I don't see Mam.

There is no place to hide as the soldiers turn drawers upside down, rip boxes apart with their bayonets, slit cushions and pillows and throw them to the floor. They tear the sheets off the beds and slit open the mattresses. They open cupboards and scoop everything out, sending dishes and glassware crashing to the floor. I hold my breath, taking little short gasps when I have to have air, and I squeeze Edith so tight, she starts to squall. Where is Mam? Marijke and René start to bawl in big boohoos.

"Shut up!" I say, and they quiet down to a whimper. I do not want the soldiers to notice us. Mam darts from her bedroom into ours. What is she doing?

My father runs from soldier to soldier. His mouth opens and closes, but nothing comes out. The soldiers knock him aside with their rifle butts. I am afraid they will use the bayonets if he doesn't stay out of their way. He can do nothing to stop them.

Finally he steps in front of a soldier who is reaching for René's teddy bear.

"Why are you doing this?" he yells. "We haven't done anything wrong!"

The soldier kicks my father in the stomach and shouts, "Satu salah, semuah salah."

When one is guilty, all are guilty.

Guilty of what?

As suddenly as they came, they are gone, along with my father who is marched out the door by one soldier just ahead of the other soldier's bayonet. The Protectors of Asia have just left us fatherless and turned our household into four rooms full of broken glass and shredded upholstery.

"Papi! Papi!" I scream, but terror grabs my throat and no sound escapes.

I guess my story—the one I always wanted to tell him—started at that very moment.

Chapter 7.
To the Camp

My mother's intuition again came into play. How could she have foreseen what was to come, this refined woman who played lawn tennis, who presided over garden parties and who played classical duets with her husband—she on the piano and he on the violin? What part of her university education prepared her to do exactly the right thing at this bizarre juncture of her life?

While we children had been rooted to the spot behind the overturned couch in the corner of the living room, and while my father had been leaping about between the rampaging soldiers, my mother had begun to throw things into pillow cases—clothing, linens, soap, candles, food, whatever we could carry that would become useful in ways even she could not have predicted. And, of course, the sewing kit.

❦

Mam rushes in from our bedroom. She ties together the ends of a long batik shawl and hangs it from her shoulder, across her body, to create a *slendang* for Edith. She takes the baby from my arms and slips her into the sling. Edith is happier now, and she snuggles against Mam's hip. Marijke, René and I creep out from behind the sofa. My whole body is shaking. René and Marijke cling to Mam.

"Ilse, put the clean *luiers* into this." Mam hands me a pillowcase. It is already heavy, but I stuff in the clean diapers while she brings more bulging pillowcases from the bedroom.

"Children, get your good shoes and put them on."

"Mami, it's too hot—" René and Marijke begin to complain.

"Do as I say!" Mam barks at us. "Quickly! They will be back." We run to do her bidding.

We are sliding into our shoes when the commotion begins again in the hallway. Mam hands the lightest pillowcase to Marijke.

"Here, my pet, you must help Mami and Ilse today," she says. "You are a big girl now." At six years old Marijke is not a very big girl, but she watches Mam and me heave our pillow case duffel bags over our shoulders—one for me and two for Mam—and she does the same. I think we must look like Black Peter's men, but it doesn't seem at all funny.

"Isoge, isoge," a soldier at our doorway screams at us. Hurry up! Mam puts both bags over one shoulder and swings René onto her free hip. Then we join our frightened neighbors being pushed down the hall and out the back door by gun barrels, bayonets, and shouting soldiers. Marijke stays behind Mam, close enough to step on her heels. Mam must put René down, and she tells him to hold onto her skirt. I come along behind Marijke, keeping her and René between Mam and me.

I know it is up to me, now, to help Mam take care of the children.

The soldiers continue to shout directions we cannot understand. But we understand the swinging rifles and bayonets, and we keep moving. As we round the side of the building we see hundreds of people being pushed into lines that lead to the trucks at the front entrance of the hotel. Something is going on at the head of the lines. We hear people screaming and crying.

Mam and I look for Pap. We can't see anything but human beings in front of us, behind us and beside us, and not one of them is Pap. Most of them are looking for someone, too, and calling out.

"Henk, Henk," my mother shouts, over and over. "Hendrik Evelijn Veere," she yells as loud as she can. Again, "Hen-drik Eh-vuh-LAYN Veere!" But Pap does not answer. A soldier thrusts his bayonet toward Mam and shouts at her. The crowd around us gets quieter, and Mam does not call out any more.

As we get closer to the head of our line, we see what is causing the weeping and the shouting. The soldiers are separating the families: men and older boys to the left, women and children to the right. Our family has already been split apart, so when we get to the head of the line, we five go off to an open truck on the right without any crying or protesting. Mam tosses the pillowcase bundles onto the open tailgate and reaches for one of the helping hands ready to pull her and Edith up into the truck. I lift René and Marijke to her, and then Mam's strong arm pulls me into the truck.

The adults—all women—sit on the benches along the sides, and the children are on the floor, sitting as close as possible to their mothers. Little ones whimper and sob. "Shush, shush, it will be all right," they are told by their mothers, but it is not very convincing, since most of the mothers are crying, too. Two Japanese guards climb in and pull up the tailgate.

The ride is short. I think we are not far from Surabaya. The truck drives through a gate, and all we can see are long, low buildings. They are barracks, Mam says. We have to stand in a line that leads up to some Javanese men who are seated at tables. They are dressed in uniforms. Mam says we have to check in.

"Like when we go to a hotel?" I ask Mam. She and the lady behind her laugh, but they don't look like they think anything is funny.

We are hoping to see Pap, but we don't see any men at all.

"Do you think they took Pap to one of those work camps?" I ask.

"I think that might be exactly where he went."

I know Mam is worried about Pap, so I don't ask any more questions that might upset her. She talks to some of the other women who are standing in line.

"This is a *doorgang*," one says.

I know what a doorgang is—a place to stay until your real place is ready. A half-way house, I've heard it called. Good. I'm glad we won't be here very long. This place is ugly. When we get to the head of the line, we are given the number of a building and the number of a room. When we find our room, another family is already there.

"Oh, I'm so sorry," Mam apologizes. "I must have gotten the wrong number."

"You got the right number," the woman says. "We're room-mates. I'm Janice." Mam introduces herself and us. We find out the other kids' names. They seem friendly, and I'm hoping they might have a game of *bikkelen*, as I left mine at De Hotel.

The room is tiny but clean, and we each have a cot with a cotton blanket. As we put our pillowcase bundles under the cots, we hear the sound of a gong.

"That means dinner," says the other lady. "The food here is not bad."

I realize I am very, very hungry.

We are lying on our cots and everyone is asleep except Mam and me. I love having Mam to myself. It makes me feel very grown up. We whisper, like girls who stay overnight at each other's houses.

"I wish we were still at De Hotel," I tell her.

"Yes, my love. I wish we were still there, too, with Pap."

"I still don't understand why we had to leave."

Mam doesn't answer right away, as if she is thinking about what she should tell me.

"Well, my pet, some people hid things in the hotel basement, things that were not allowed."

"What things?"

"Oh, radios and telegraph transmitters and guns. Things like that."

I could understand why guns would not be allowed, but I had to ask, "What is wrong with radios and telegraph transmitters?"

"The Japanese do not want us to be in contact with the outside world, darling—with their enemies."

"I suppose their enemies are our friends."

"Yes, I suppose," she agreed.

"And they might be able to help us, if we could get in touch with them." I think I have figured it out, and Mam agrees.

"But Mam, we didn't hide anything, did we?"

"Surely not, pet. We are blameless."

A thought occurred to me that made me sit up straight. "Mam, would we still be at De Hotel if it weren't for the people who hid those things?"

"Probably so."

"Then why didn't the Japs just take them and leave us alone? I hate those people!"

"Hush, hush, Ilse. You must try not to hate. They were doing what they thought was right." Mam is a Christian, and she always teaches us the Christian way of looking at things.

"Well, then, can I hate the ones who told the Japanese about the hidden things?"

Mam sighs. "What do you think, Ilse?"

"I suppose they thought they were doing the right thing, too."

Mam leans across the narrow space between our cots, to kiss my cheek.

"Mam?"

"Yes, my love?"

"Can I hate the Japs?"

Chapter 8.
Introduction to Camp Halmaheira

I do not remember the name of that first camp, our first taste of life behind barbed wire and high fences. I do remember we turned out for roll call every morning, and we were required to bow when we saw our oppressors who occasionally screamed or barked at us. But they did not mistreat us, and I do not remember being hungry at the doorgang. Just as we had adjusted to life in De Hotel, we adjusted to life in prison. After a few short weeks we were ordered into trucks. Again, the children were relegated to the floorboards. I am sure I argued that since I was ten years old, I should be considered an adult. It didn't work. This trip was a long one.

Our destination turned out to be a concentration camp for women and children on the outskirts of Semarang, a large city on the north central coast of Java. Camp Halmaheira had been one of those large neighborhoods built for *koolies,* manual laborers, with hundreds of humble little houses rowed up and down paved streets. All dirt and pavement, no lawns or gardens. Since we were prisoners, not koolies, the camp was surrounded by a high, solid *gedek*—a fence of woven bamboo. Armed guards were everywhere. We would learn later that the camp was commanded by the Kempeitai, our misfortune.

The trucks pulled through the iron gate late at night. I remember being grateful that the journey was ended, thinking anything would be better than rattling around in the bottom of a truck.

We tumble out of our truck as fast as we can, and Mam hands down the pillowcase bundles. Our two guards line us up and start us walking—one of them is up front and the other is at the rear of the line. It is dark, but dim street lamps light our way.

"*Isoge, isoge*," our guards are yelling. I understand some of the words now, especially the one that means "Hurry up!" I can hardly walk after so many hours on the truck floor, and I have to go to the bathroom.

René is shuffling along, half asleep, and I have to prod him to go faster. I can't pick him up. Edith is crying in the slendang, and Marijke is whining. "I'm hungry, Mami. I can't carry the pillowcase. I'm tired."

I have to carry my pillowcase and hers too. And does she think she's the only one who is hungry? I wish I could slap Marijke, and I wish we could slow down.

We pass one house after another; they all look alike. There is something strange about them. When our guard stops in front of one of them, I realize what is strange.

"Mam, Mam, there is no door on this house," I whisper. "You can see right in."

We all stand there in the bare dirt, staring at the little bungalow. A soldier jabs Mam's shoulder several times with his hand. "*Kapala kongsie*," he says. House mother? We have to walk by him to enter the house. He says words that I think are counting words: "Ichi, ni, san, shi..."

I count too, in Dutch, while I wait my turn to go in. "Ein, twee, drie, vier..." There are thirty-nine of us. I wonder how so many people can be expected to live in one tiny little house. Perhaps this is just the first stop because it is late. Probably we will move into our own house tomorrow. Someone finds a switch and a dim light goes on in the middle of the ceiling of the front room.

There are no doors inside, either—just open doorframes where doors used to be. And no furniture at all, just sleeping mats stacked up on the floor. We drag our pillow cases into the first bedroom and put them down by a tall window with a deep sill. Edith quiets down when Mam takes her out of the slendang and rocks her, side to side.

Mam speaks loudly so everyone can hear. "Let's take the mattresses and find a place to sleep. Keep your families together. In the morning we will find out more about this place and what needs to be done."

Everyone starts doing what she says, and I am very proud of her for being the leader.

Mam and I carry three sleeping mats to the place by the tall window. It is a good place, I think. We can put things on the sill, and we can see out the window when we start feeling cooped up like chickens. But the mattresses are something else—even in the dim light we can see disgusting stains, and the smell makes me gag. Mam pulls some of the bed linens from our pillow case bundles and spreads them over the mattresses. It doesn't help much. And we all need to pee.

"Aieee!" we hear a woman shout from the room that has the toilet. "It is plugged up with something." One by one we all go to look at the toilet, and she is right. It is plugged up with something that looks like concrete. Family by family, we go outside to find a place to relieve ourselves. We do not know what else to do. Thank heaven, it is dark.

"Mami, I am hungry," whines Marijke.

Mam digs into the slendang. It is not only Edith's cozy place, but it is a pocket to hide goodies for times like this. She pulls out two overripe, darkly speckled bananas and divides them between the three of us.

"Here, Mam, take mine." I am not being generous. I just feel sick at my stomach from the awful odors of this house and my mattress.

Mam closes her eyes and shakes her head. "You will sleep better if you eat it," she says.

I choke it down and she is right. I am grateful to be on a stationary floor, not one that has little metal ridges and rolls along over rough pavement, bump, bump, bump. I am very, very sleepy.

I waken to the sound of a gong. I feel the tones as well as hear them. Bong! Bong! The sun is rising, so it must be about six o'clock.

"Get ready for roll call," Mam calls to everyone. We know, from our last camp, what is expected.

We all line up in front of our house. When the guard shouts, "*Keirei*"—bow down—we are already making the required deep bow, body bent at the hip, head down, hands at our sides. Then we hear the prisoners in front of the house next door counting down—in Japanese! We don't know the Japanese numbers.

The guard stands in front of us and we bow again. Mam is the first in line.

"Satu," she says, the Bahasa Maleis word for "one."

The guard slaps her face so hard her head jerks sideways. Then he slaps the other side, which jerks her head the other way. My eyes pop wide open and I gasp to see such a thing happen to Mam, but then I get slapped, too. All of the adults and older children get the same treatment. At least he leaves the little ones alone. I want to cry, I feel so helpless, but I am too frightened to make a sound. I hold my breath. Then the guard comes back to Mam and slaps her again, twice. Is it her fault we do not know how to count in Japanese?

Oh, my face stings, and poor Mam has big, red finger-shaped welts rising up on her cheeks. An Indies woman from the house next door comes over to Mam. She looks nice, and her eyes show she is sorry about the red welts. I think she must be the kapala kongsie from the next house.

"Come with me," she says. "I will show you the community toilets."

"Good." Mam looks grateful. "We are in need! Come, children." We take a few steps, but then Mam stops and turns back. She probably remembers she is the kapala kongsie and has a duty to the others. "Come! Come!" she calls. "We will visit the toilets." She is a very good kapala kongsie, I think.

The rest of them line up behind us—mostly Hollanders, but also some Indies, like us. I must remember not to use the word "cheesehead" for Hollanders. It is not polite. Off we go to find a place to pee. The only islanders I see are some Javanese men in green jumpsuits. They seem to be workers or perhaps even guards, but not prisoners. I guess it is only the Dutch and the partly Dutch who are enemies of the Japanese.

"Why are the toilets in the houses filled with concrete?" asks one of the Hollanders as we walk along.

"They are afraid we might escape," answers the other kapala kongsie.

"Escape?" several of us say.

"Yes," she answers. "The toilets all drained into a sewer ditch that used to run through the camp. It emptied into the river over there." She points to one side of the camp where I guess a river must flow outside the bamboo fence. "They drained the ditch because we could jump into it and swim out to the river."

"Ugh!" I say. "I cannot imagine why ANYONE would jump into such a ditch."

The woman turns her head and gives me a hard look. "You will learn, girl," she says. Her voice is harsh, and I feel embarrassed. We keep on walking. The toilets seem to be quite a long way from our house, perhaps eight or ten blocks.

At last we come to an open area of what looks like a line of cement boxes in the ground. They are oblong, about as long as Mam's arm and maybe half as wide. I can't tell how deep they are. One or two boards are lying across the top of each hole. Flies are everywhere, covering the boards and swarming in black clouds. I look across the line of holes, wondering what they are, when suddenly I understand what I am seeing. In spite of the flies, my jaw drops open.

"Mam!"

Mam's mouth is open, too. We are looking at women, their feet on boards, their bottoms bare, squatting over the open holes. Right there in front of everyone, with soldiers looking on. I cannot bear their shame, and I turn and bury my head in the side of Mam's soft bosom.

These are the squatting holes according to the woman who brought us here, the only toilets available to us. Some of the women and children in our group have such urgent need, they step up on boards and squat.

Never, I think. Never will I do such a thing in public.

We return to our bungalow. We follow Mam around to the side of the house where we find an open cesspool of gray water between our house and the next. Grass grows around the murky pool, a green spot in the midst of dirt-brown ugliness.

"Here, children," says Mam. "We can make a little circle, for privacy, and take turns squatting here in the grass."

We do as she says. I envy René, as he doesn't have to squat. From the smell, we can tell we are not the only ones who have used this place for this purpose. And it is not very private.

Mam reads my mind. "I think we will have to get used to the public toilets," she says.

Then, as a good kapala kongsie, Mam tells us she is going next door to find someone to teach us the Japanese numerals up to thirty-nine. I guess we will not be moving into a house of our own.

Chapter 9.
Porridge and Swill

Food was served twice a day at Halmaheira. We trudged to the central kitchen shortly after the 6:00 AM sunrise, and again at sunset, 6:00 PM. Our captors fed us just enough to keep us alive, but not enough to keep us healthy. Food would become an obsession that controlled my life. It was not a matter of feeling satisfied or comfortable. It was a matter of survival. Prisoners suffered from malnutrition and weakness, not to mention diarrhea, beriberi, dysentery, infections, and the organ malfunctions that accompany inadequate diet. During our entire imprisonment—over two years—the menu never varied. It was the same each day as it had been that very first day.

⟡

I am recovered enough from the shock of seeing the camp toilets to notice I am hungry. "When will we have breakfast?" I ask. The sun is by now full in the sky.

"Soon," Mam tells me. "We will take our bowls to the kitchen, just as we did at the doorgang, and bring our food back to the house."

At the last camp, we had tables to sit at. I wonder where we will eat at this place. All the space is taken up with sleeping mats, suitcases, and bundles of belongings. It is very crowded. And even if we had tables and benches where everyone could sit, we have been told it is against the rules to gather in a group— a *kumpulan*. This, I think, is going to be hard in a tiny house with thirty-nine people. How can we avoid being together? But Mam says we must obey the rules, and she is the kapala kongsie.

When the camp residents begin to move toward the middle of the camp, we join them. We each have a wooden bowl in hand. I carry Edith's bowl. Even though she is only a baby, we hope she will get a full ration. Maybe they will have a special nutritious custard for babies. Mam has not been able to nurse her, so Edith must eat whatever liquids and soft gruel her little baby throat can swallow.

I have never seen such long lines. We cannot even see where our line ends. I would like to visit with the other people in line—some look to be my age. Guards are all over the place, and I think if we are not supposed to get together in the house, we are probably not supposed to get together out here, either. I will ask Mam about that later. I am glad the line moves fast.

When we get closer, I see huge steel cook pots the size of oil drums standing on wheels outside the gate of an outdoor kitchen. I watch the others so I will know what to do. We approach one of the cook pots, and I see a ladle about the size of my cupped hand scoop something that looks like porridge out of the pot and plop it into an outstretched bowl. The line never stops. Plop, plop, don't stop, I think, and I hold two bowls out. The server looks up. She is a prisoner, a Hollander, and she has red rings around her eyes. She must be very tired.

"One for the baby," Mam explains, pointing to Edith in the slendang. She does not ask about custard. The server nods, and I get a plop in each bowl.

We hurry back to the house. The weather is pleasant, so we join our housemates outside on the *platje,* a patch of concrete that is probably supposed to be a verandah, or maybe a patio. It is too small for either one. Mam points to one side of the square, and we sit there with our butts on concrete and our legs stuck out in the bare dust. I guess this does not count as a kumpulan.

Marijke, René and I bow our heads. Mam makes the blessing short. "Dear Father, thank you for the food we are about to eat. Please take care of Henk and keep him safe. In Jesus' name we pray. Amen." Always, in every prayer, we ask God to take care of Pap.

Then I scoop up my first taste of Halmaheira rice porridge—*bubur dedek*—with brown rice husks mixed in. It does not taste good—no nutmeg sprinkled on the top, nor thick sweet coconut cream poured over it. But I am very hungry and I eat it quickly. I look at Mam who is poking the gruel into Edith's mouth, trying to avoid the brown husks. Marijke and I speak at the same time.

"Mam, I am still hungry." We are a duet, and little René nods his head. "Me, too," he says. He is a very sweet three-and-a-half-year old, and right now he looks so pitiful I feel like crying.

Mam divides her portion among the three of us. I feel guilty for taking her food. I notice when Edith is finished, Mam eats all the husks that are left in the bowl. I decide that from now on I will not take any of Mam's food. Besides, it doesn't help much. I am still hungry.

I stay that way until dinner which turns out to be a ladle of white rice—no husks this time—two ladles of watery soup, and a fresh red pepper. Everyone gets the same. When the lady hands the long red pepper to Edith who grasps the pretty thing in her little hand, I laugh and try to pull it away from her to give it back. Mam nudges me along.

"Mam, the baby can't eat that pepper!" I whisper.

"Of course not, darling. But we can. Move along, now." We return to the house. It is almost dark, so we go indoors and make a family circle on our mattresses. Mam blesses the food, and we are ready to eat our first Halmaheira supper.

René lifts his bowl and slurps his soup, which floats above the rice. His face scrunches into a point in the middle. "Mami, what is this?"

Mam sips her soup. She tilts her head and narrows her eyes down, like she's thinking. "Well, I'd call it vegetable soup."

A lady close by says, "If you want to be truthful, call it swill."

It looks and tastes like cloudy water to me, but I find the point end of a cooked carrot, my favorite vegetable. I drink the swill, whatever that is, down to the rice and then use my fingers to scoop the rice into my mouth as slowly as I can. Perhaps it will last longer in my stomach if I take longer to eat it. Then it is time for the red pepper.

"Mami, do I bite into it?" Marijke asks. We have never eaten raw red peppers whole, with the seeds and all. Babu kokki always roasted them or cut them into small pieces to add to other foods. But we have no way to roast them, and no other foods to add them to.

Mam snaps the pepper in half and shakes the loose seeds out onto a handkerchief she uses as a napkin. She sticks her finger inside the pepper, to loosen the attached seeds, and she gives both halves a sharp shake. "Here, try this," she says.

We watch Marijke bite off a chunk of the pepper. She chews, and suddenly a red mess comes flying out of her mouth. She is coughing and tears are flowing. René's eyes get very wide, and he throws his pepper down on the floor. By this time, Marijke is crying in loud boohoos. I try not to laugh at her, but I can't help it. Mam picks her up and soothes her.

"I guess you have to get used to red peppers," Mam says when Marijke is finally quiet. "They are good for us. They have many vitamins and will prevent scurvy. But for now, you may have this." Mam reaches into her deep slendang pocket and pulls out a little bit of carrot which seems to me to be a very fine trade for a hot pepper. It also seems like magic, the way she always has a tidbit for us at just the right time. She puts another piece of carrot in René's hand and picks his red pepper up off the floor.

It is my turn to try the red pepper. I prepare it as Mam had done. After the first two or three bites, my mouth has gone numb, but I like the feel of the skin as I bite through it, and I can stand the heat. Mam finishes Marijke's pepper as I finish mine. She puts the three remaining peppers into her pocket. "These will be snacks when we are hungry," she says.

I do not tell her, but I am already hungry.

Chapter 10.
Everyday Torture

It was our misfortune that Halmaheira was one of the camps run by the Kempeitai, the military police unit of the Japanese army, sometimes called the Japanese "Gestapo." I doubt if any of us understood the real power of the Kempeitai outside our own miserable existence at Camp Halmaheira. They were feared and hated, even in Japan. Trained in torture methods, their brutality was legendary.

The Kempeitai carried swords—I called them Samurai swords, named for the Samurai warriors who once used them. The enlisted soldiers carried *shinai*, bamboo swords. The swords were their signature weapon as an elite group, and whether they were bamboo or steel, they served as instruments for beating. The Kempeitai wielded billy clubs as well, but for everyday brutality their specialty was kicking. "Watch out for the boots," we were warned early on.

For an ordinary offense like failing to bow low enough when we crossed paths with a Japanese soldier, we might get a single kick to the belly or the shin. For serious offenses, it was much worse. And the rules were clear: when a punishment took place, all who were within sight of it must watch in silence and refrain from giving aid of any kind. They must bow to show respect for the punisher and regret for the crime, no matter who had committed it. After all, "Satu salah, semuah salah!" When one is guilty, all are guilty.

No one was safe from their shiny, steel-toed combat boots. Combat, indeed—against helpless women and innocent children. Of course there were other punishments, too. Oh dear God, such punishments.

It is time to see what our neighborhood has to offer. Mam won't let any of us out of her sight, so I wait until everyone lies down to take a nap, and then I slip away. I am hoping to find some food. All the snacks in Edith's slendang are used up—mostly to keep Marijke from whining—and I am hungry. Very, very hungry. I think I will have quite a bit of freedom to move about the camp if I just keep my head down and act like I have someplace to go. I know I am taking a chance of catching it from both Mam and a Kempeitai boot, but it will be worth it if I come home with something to eat.

I walk to the end of our block and turn the corner just in time to see a guard lift his sword, sheath and all, and knock a woman to the pavement. I see something fly out of her hand and fall to the street. It looks like a turnip or a rutabaga. I want to turn and run, but I am afraid to call attention to myself.

"No, no, please," she cries, holding her hands to her face and curling her body around like a snail's shell. The guard shouts at her and begins the kicking. He turns his shoulders, like he is winding up, and then with a loud "unff" he throws his whole body forward as he swings his boot into her back, her head, her legs. Then he walks around to kick her in the stomach, the chest, the face. Her body lifts up with each kick. She stops screaming between the kicks, and just makes a groaning sound each time the boot lands. I feel myself groaning, too, inside. I am too scared to make a sound. Blood is coming out of her head.

When she stops moving and groaning, the soldier stops the torture and straightens his uniform. He looks in my direction. By now I am locked to the spot, shaking, unable to move or look away from the broken, bloody woman on the street. I know I should try to help her, but all I can do is stand here, hanging my head, kind of huddled up inside myself like I'm trying to hide right out here in plain view. I am too afraid to raise my head or make a move.

The soldier grunts something. I think he may be saying, "Let this be a lesson." I see his boot come down over the thing that had fallen to the street, and he crushes it to pulp. When he leaves, two women run out of their house, scrape up the mess and eat it on the spot. Then they pick up the woman who is lying in the street and carry her off to their house. She leaves a trail of blood.

It is only when I stop shaking enough to walk back to the house that I remember the rules: watch in silence, bow head, and give no assistance to the one being punished. I have followed them perfectly; my fear has saved me. I go home and slip back onto my mat, but I cannot close my eyes because when I do I see the woman bleeding in the street.

I am changing Edith's luier. Oh, it is foul. Poor little thing, the diarrhea just pours from her. What a time for Mam to be gone to the squatting holes with René.

"Hand me the wet cloth," I say to Marijke, who is trying to help, but she gags with the smell of the diaper and makes me gag, too.

Bong! Bong! Oh, no. The gong is calling us to a special roll call, or to the big square for a punishment. It never calls us to anything good, and I'm not sure what to do without Mam. I can't do anything until I get a clean diaper on this baby.

Everyone in the house is lined up by the time I get the diaper fastened. I hike Edith up on my hip and take Marijke by the hand.

"Come," I say. "You must stay quiet and not call attention to us."

But we are already attracting attention by being late to line up. We take our places, leaving Mam's and Rene's spots open. It is very important that we stand in our assigned spots. We could be kicked for being out of place. We bow low, as always, and then stand at attention. A soldier appears in front of me, his eyes are flashing danger, I think. I stand as straight as I can. I wish Edith would stop squirming, and I hope Marijke will not start crying. Where is Mam?

The soldier has the same question. He growls at me. "*Kapala kongsie-wa dokoda?*"

I am grateful that I understand the question, but I have no words to answer. I don't know what to do, so I squat, stick out my rear end, and point in the direction of the toilets. The soldier's face twists, and I am sure I am going to be kicked. He bares his long teeth and, surprise of all surprises, he laughs and turns away.

My legs go rubbery, and I have to make myself hold onto Edith and keep standing. Marijke has been frightened into a starched little stick figure, and that's how Mam finds us when she and René return to take their places in line. Mam takes Edith from my arms and puts her into the slendang.

"Thank you," she says with her eyes. No talking allowed.

The hot sun takes the strength right out of our bodies, but we have to stand straight. Those who fall down are beaten with the flat side of a samurai sword, or kicked. The bedbugs by now are not just a night time plague. They have burrowed into the seams of our clothing. It is impossible not to scratch the bites until they bleed. Salt from my sweat runs into the open wounds, and now I have stinging to go along with the itching. But still we stand in line. How long can this go on?

"*Naore! Naore!*" the guards shout. Stand up straight! And we do it, or we get the boot.

René, next to Mam, begins to sway. Even though we are supposed to look straight ahead, I sneak sideways glances at him. His eyes are rolling up under his lids. Surely they will not kick a little boy. Just as his legs give out, Mam lifts him to her hip. There she stands, straight as a lamp post, with a baby on one hip, a three-year-old on the other, and tears streaming from her eyes. Even though I may be beaten, I cannot take my eyes from her beautiful face.

Then Marijke, who has been so brave, begins to whimper. "Mami, I have to pee."

Our guard glares and takes a step toward Marijke. Mam's mouth flies open, and she sucks in her breath. I reach over to squeeze Marijke's shoulder. There is nothing else to be done, so Marijke pees right there in line.

At dusk, when we should be going to eat, we are sent into our houses. No dinner. What have we been guilty of today? Who knows? I go straight to my mattress and fall onto it, sick and exhausted from standing all day under a blistering sun.

Chapter 11.
The Tea House Draft

The Kempeitai who ran our camp lived in well-appointed quarters up a low rise from the rest of the village, always in view from the street in front of our house. Their houses looked much like ours, but with doors and privacy and, most certainly, with toilets. No open filth holes for our captors. They also had lawns. We saw green-suited Javanese men tending the grounds, beating dust from the soldiers' sleeping mats, moving from building to building to maintain the comfort of the Japanese. One of the buildings was called the Tea House. We learned about the Tea House draft in the early weeks of our residency at Camp Halmaheira.

❧

Maybe if I pound my mattress hard enough with this broken down old bamboo *sapulidi* I will be able to squash the bedbugs as well as lift out the dust. It is so hot this afternoon, and my bites seem even worse than usual.

Bong! Bong! Oh, no, not another roll call. I will faint this time, for sure. I wish I could just lie back down with the bedbugs, but that is impossible. I pick up Edith and carry her to the lineup. Mam nudges Marijke and René along in front of her.

A woman I have never seen hurries past my mother. "Tea House draft," she whispers. "Take the baby, quickly. You will not be considered a prize so soon after giving birth. And tell your big girl to act sick."

Tea House draft? What could that be? I wish I could ask Mam, but I have missed my chance. We are not allowed to talk.

Soldiers stroll back and forth, stroking their chins as if in deep thought. They stop in front of some women to look up and down their bodies. I feel very uncomfortable with this. They snort and laugh as they make their choices. They point at a woman or a young girl. "*Omae*," they grunt. "You." They pull her out of line and point to a place where she is to stand. From other lineups, we hear sobbing, but no slapping or kicking. I think they do not want to damage their picks—I am beginning to suspect what this is about.

One of the soldiers is looking in my direction and my breath stops. I know I do not want to be chosen to step out of line, so I pretend cramping in my stomach. I bend a little bit in my middle and pretend that I am trying to keep from groaning. The corners of the soldier's mouth turn down, and he moves on. He also passes by my mother. Two young women are chosen from our house, and they follow the soldiers up the block toward Headquarters Hill.

We are dismissed. Mam hugs me. "You are a very smart girl," she says, and I go back to pounding my sleeping mat.

Mam is not so strict any more, thank heaven. She lets me go to the squatting holes by myself, so I pretend I must go often. Then

I meander around, scavenging for food. It occupies much of my time, and I find I have a talent for it. I wear coveralls with pockets to hold my finds. I carry handkerchiefs to stuff on top of the forbidden haul, both to hide it, and in some cases to keep it from escaping. I have already learned that anything that crawls, you can eat.

I have been watching a row of banana trees growing on the edge of the Kempeitai lawns. They have been in bloom, and I can't wait to see if little fruits have appeared yet. I stroll up the street, my head down as usual, as if I am walking home. As I approach the trees, I see that the blossoms have been picked.

My eyes are full of tears. Now there will be no fruit, and I was hoping to surprise Mam with a pocketful of baby bananas. Oh, well, perhaps not all is lost. The blossom thief may not know about the fat grubs that live in the folds of the leaves next to the tree trunk. I peel back the big leaves and I am rewarded. I fill my pocket with big white worms. Oh, bananas would have been so delicious. My eyes get full again, and I start to cry. But I must be quiet about it.

As I turn toward home I realize I am not the only one crying. I hear a woman sobbing. Loud! I know I should run away fast, but I am too curious. I follow the sound to a lean-to built against a shed just inside the Kempeitai compound.

As I near the shed, I hear men grunting and laughing. I peek through the slats of the lean-to and see soldiers holding a woman down on some kind of table. Is this the blossom thief? Soldiers are pinning her arms and holding her legs apart. One of them stands between her spread legs, zipping his trousers. I know enough about sex between a man and a woman to know that what is going on here is not right, and I turn and run as fast as I can. I don't dare make a sound.

"Mam, Mam," I call as soon as I get home. I pour out the story of what I saw.

"What were you doing there, you naughty girl?" Mam's jaw gets tight, and the look she gives me feels like stinging bullets.

"Uh, the, the, uh, banana trees," I stammer. I am caught, and Mam is angry.

Then Mam bursts into tears and hugs me tight, and I know she is worried, not angry. I forget about the worms in my pocket, I am so overcome with guilt for worrying my mother.

"Ilse, you must promise me you will never go near the Kempeitai headquarters again. It is too dangerous. They could have gotten YOU in that shed."

I promise, but it is a promise I will never keep. I am always too hungry, and even if I never get a baby banana, the grubs are plentiful.

I wake one morning, and Mam tells me to remove my shirt and raise my arms. This is puzzling, but I do as she says. She takes a root of some kind out of her pocket, and she rubs the cut end over my armpits. It feels cool, damp against my skin. Whatever is she doing?

"You may feel a little sick, pet, but it won't last long. It is better this way," she says. "You are a beautiful girl."

By the time we fall out for roll call, I am sweating, and I think my skin looks yellow. I don't feel very beautiful!

My sister, Marijke, says the magical root was simply an onion, but we would have eaten anything as delectable as an onion. Whatever it was, it stank. I stank. It never left my mother's pocket, and I was never molested or chosen for Tea House duty. And never, in all my life, has hair grown in the pits of my arms.

Chapter 12.
Extraordinary Torture

Exchanging goods over the bamboo wall was a serious crime at Camp Halmaheira. Mam's pillow cases held premium tradables—linen napkins, for instance, with embroidered edging. The destitute Javanese treasured such items and could be coaxed into tossing food over the fence in return for a pretty dress or fine linens. Negotiations were tricky. First of all, we could not see through the thick, woven bamboo. With whom were we negotiating? Japanese collaborators? There were plenty of those on the free side of the fence. Once a safe contact was made and a deal struck, which side of the trade would be tossed over the fence first?

"Throw the food first," Mam would demand, and when the precious foodstuff came sailing over the fence, she would toss away the dress or the embroidered tablecloth or the silk undergarment that had been bargained for in whispers. It had to be wadded up tightly, to clear the top of the fence.

Mam's shrewdness paid off, both in stuffing those pillowcases in the first place and in her choice of contacts on the other side of the fence. But they were not generous. Our pillowcase treasury dwindled.

I left the black marketeering to Mam, but I was always fearful for her, especially after I witnessed a particularly cruel punishment.

❦

I am on my way home from the squatting holes. I round a corner and see several Indies women near the fence being slapped by two Japanese. They are crying, "*Ampun! Ampun!*" Forgive me! Forgive me! I see a beautiful beaded shawl stuck on the top of the fence, and I know what has happened.

"No, no, no," cries one of the women. "I do not have any fruit. I was just walking by."

The guard screams at her and knocks her to the ground. A *djeruk bali* falls out from under her skirt and rolls away. In spite of myself, my attention is drawn to the thick-skinned, over-sized grapefruit, and my saliva begins to run as my tastebuds remember the sweet taste of the juicy red meat.

The guard begins to kick the woman. "I am sorry, I am sorry," she screams, but he keeps right on kicking. Camp rules say I must stay here and watch. Thank heaven I have nothing in my pockets today.

The other women bow low and hand their fruit over. They are saying things like, "I am sorry for my crime." "I deserve punishment." "I am dirt under your feet." Sometimes when a prisoner admits she has done something wrong and begs the guards to forgive her, they will give her a cigarette or a sweet treat to show how "goodhearted" they are. But not this time.

I hear the gong calling everyone to come and see what happens to people who trade their belongings for food. I stand still as a wax figure and wait for the others to gather in a big circle around the frightened women. I look for my mother, and I see her on the other side of the circle. I do not dare to go to her, but our eyes meet, and we nod to each other ever so slightly. We could be kicked for not paying attention to the punishment.

When the kicking and the beating are over, the women bend forward at the hip. One by one, the guards put heavy bamboo poles in the crooks behind their knees, and then they make the women sit back on their heels. I wonder why. One of them has dysentery. She must be so humiliated, but there is nothing she can do but let it go.

We are not dismissed. It is going to be one of those long afternoons in the hot sun, just standing and waiting. I am glad I went to the toilet. I let my mind drift, and I think about the *dokars* we used to ride, those horse-drawn buggies that are connected to the horse's harness by long poles that don't bend when the horse falls down. In the hilly cities where we have lived, the horses are always falling down. When that happens, the back end of the dokar flies up. You feel like you are going to sail right out, over the horse. This, I am sure is where I get my horse phobia. Worse yet, the poor horse whinnies and twists about. I am always afraid it won't be able to get back up and someone will have to come and shoot it. That's what Pap says you have to do to a horse that breaks its leg. I don't like horses, but I don't want them to be shot, either

"Papi, could we please walk?" I would always ask.

"Don't be silly, Ilse," he would answer. "We are going across town."

"Well, then, a *bedjak*," I would say.

"Nonsense!" Pap did not like to ride in those pedaled taxis with a bench across the back. He said it was undignified for a man of stature to have another man cart him about on a tricycle. Pap was always concerned about dignity. His dignity wouldn't last long in this place. I wonder if he is in a camp like this one. Maybe he works somewhere for the Japanese. Pap is very strong. Maybe he has gone to the oil fields. Or maybe not.

Maybe that soldier with the bayonet, but no, I cannot let my thoughts go in that direction.

Oh, how I wish I could get into a dokar right now and be pulled out of here.

The sun goes down and dinner time goes by. I am hungry and I want to cry, but I don't want to annoy the guards. Finally, the bamboo poles are pulled away and the women are told to stand up. They scream, fall, and roll on the ground, still screaming. I am so surprised, I almost scream, too. We are sent home in silence, without dinner.

When all in the house are in their places for the night and it is dark, Mam produces a djeruk bali. We must be careful, as we do not want the other people in the house to know we have food. She takes out the tiny knife she fashioned from a tin can and scores the rind, all the way around, cutting top to bottom, through the navel. Then again, to separate the rind into four sections. A little tug, here and there, and the rind gives way, and we have four arcs of rind—yellow on the outside, and white and pethy on the inside. I wish I could make a little wheeled cart out of the djeruk bali arcs, as Babu Kokki used to do. René would so enjoy it. But Mam will have to get rid of the evidence. She pulls the ball of fruit apart and gives us each a segment.

"Here, take small bites, and it will last longer," she whispers.

I take my first bite of the ruby fruit. Oh, it is so delicious. Mam pinches off tiny pieces to put into Edith's mouth. She licks the juice that runs down her hand. We get more segments, and for once, Mam gets to eat some, too, as the djeruk bali is big enough to share four ways, five if you count baby Edith. We all lick our hands and arms, not wanting to give up any of the sweetness of the juice.

When we have poked the last dripping pieces into our mouths, the little ones are ready to sleep. But I cannot put thoughts of today's torture out of my mind.

"Mam, what happened to those women?" I ask. "Why did they scream and fall?"

"That is what happens when the circulation is cut off for so long and then restored, my love. It causes hideous pain. You must never do anything to bring such a punishment on yourself."

I stay awake for a long time. I know that Mam took her place at the fence today. She could have been one of those women screaming in pain. What would I do if such a thing ever happened to Mam? I am shaking and crying, and I climb over Edith to get to Mam's mat. She moves over to give me room to lie beside her, and she puts her arms around me. I am sobbing too hard to speak. She holds me and pets me until I am calm and I can tell her what is on my mind.

"Oh, Mam, please do not go to the fence again, ever," I say.

"Don't worry, my precious girl. I will not put myself in danger."

But I know she will. Her fear of watching us starve is greater than her fear of being punished.

There it goes again, the gong. This time the guards are out in the street herding us to the community square. This is for serious public punishment; sometimes women are killed. I dread what is to come. We circle around the open lot. Two tall poles rise up from the packed earth, and a sturdy crossbeam stretches between them, across the top. Three Dutch women sob and beg for mercy. They had dared to take *katjang pandjang*—bundles of long green beans—from the community kitchen to give to the nuns who run the camp orphanage. Each one confesses, as we watch, to the three soldiers who are beating them with their Samurai swords.

"I am heartily sorry. I deserve the harshest punishment, even death, for what I did," says one. The prisoners always have to admit to a terrible crime, even if it is only taking a little bit of food. Not that it does any good—they are always beaten for stealing food, whether they confess or not. What do the Japanese expect, when we are all so hungry?

The real beatings begin, this time with billy clubs, and we watch because it is the rule. Finally all three women are lying flat on the ground. Their eyes are closed, but I know they are still alive because they are groaning. The guards put away their billy clubs and I think it must be over. But no, they pick up ropes that have been coiled up beside one of the poles. I am very curious now, because I have never seen a punishment performed with ropes before.

I watch as the soldiers tie each woman's feet together—each one has her own rope. They jerk hard to make the knots tight. I think it must hurt, but the women have stopped groaning. I hope they have just fainted. Then the soldiers throw the ends of the ropes over the crossbeam. "Ungh!!!" one grunts when his rope hits the beam and bounces back. The others laugh at him, and he says some words in Japanese that I know to be curse words. His rope sails over the top on his next try, and they laugh again.

Now they pull on the ends of the ropes, and the women are hauled up, feet first. The soldiers tie the rope ends to pegs sticking out of the poles and walk off, leaving the women dangling upside down in the middle of the square. I want to walk away, too, but we are not permitted. I want to look away, to cuddle up to my mother and let her hold me tight. But that is not permitted either. I just have to keep looking at the women. Their arms hang down, limp, over their heads, their fingers almost brushing the dirt. As I watch their helpless suffering, I am glad they are wearing coveralls, so their bottoms are not bared in their upside down state.

But bare bottoms would be better than what happens to them over the next few hours. Their faces swell and turn mottled reds and then purples. Their eyes pop open and bulge out. I think they must be dead.

At last, the ropes are sliced cleanly with a swish of a samurai swords. One, two, three, their bodies fall, hands first, to the ground, and we are sent home. No dinner. We are being punished for the crime of stealing green beans.

I cannot sleep. My eyes will not close over the image of those women's bloated, purple faces.

"You should not have looked, Ilse," my mother scolds. "You should have turned your eyes away."

She is right. So why did I keep looking? I was too afraid to look away, for fear they would string me upside down for disobeying the rules.

Chapter 13.
Stalking the Central Kitchen

The central kitchen was a large outdoor area where food was cooked for both the Japanese and the prisoners. Enclosed by a high barbed wire fence, it was guarded day and night by armed sentries. As if barbed wire and armed guards weren't enough, a wide ditch, like a deep, waterless moat separated us from the fence on our side of the camp. The kitchen gate was always locked, except to allow the prisoners who worked there and their guards to enter and exit, and to roll the big cooking drums out and in again at meal time.

I think, now, that the wide ditch must have been part of the dried up sewer, for *alang alang* grew thick and rich from the bottom of the ditch—tall-stemmed grass which is wide at the base and sharp on the edges. It didn't take long for me to discover that a small ten-year-old girl could maneuver easily and undetected down inside the alang alang which was almost as high as I was. I remember the hours I spent lying in the ditch, daydreaming while I watched the women prepare vegetables at large wooden tables where they peeled and pared, sliced and chopped.

❦

Turnips, carrots, cabbage, onions, parsnips, leeks—I bring my jaws together slowly and imagine how my teeth would feel, sinking down into those plump, fresh vegetables. My mouth waters as I imagine the taste coating my tongue and spreading to the sides of my mouth. The cooks' knives fly. Chop, chop. Whack, whack. These women do not look like our babu kokki, but their knives move just as fast. They toss the good parts of the vegetables into cooking pots and woks, along with beef and pork and chicken. The Japanese eat delicious food. The vegetable peelings and the raggedy tops and bottoms go into the huge drums, to be boiled and become our weak soup. No meat, ever, for us.

But I don't lie here to torture myself with the sight of food I cannot have. The cooks often drop pieces of food on the ground. When a good piece falls near the fence, it is mine. All I have to do is watch for just the right moment—when no one is look-ing my way—and I lift the wicked strand of barbed wire with one hand while the other hand darts under and brings back the treasure. On good days, it is too much to safely conceal in my pocket, so I must stack up my stolen vegetables down in the ditch under the alang alang and return for them later when the camp is quiet and not so many guards are looking for someone to punish. I always know exactly where I left my precious stash, and I know how to avoid the guards.

One of the cooks drops more food than the rest, and I think I see her knife flick the chunks toward the fence, oh so fast. She must know I am here, but she never looks at me because if she did the guards might also look my way. I don't know what would happen if they saw me. I don't think it is against the rules to lie in the ditch next to the fence. However, I'm sure it would become a rule if they caught me here. And I know what will happen if they ever catch me when I come back later. The purple faces of the upside down women come to me and a shudder starts at my neck and shakes me all the way to my toes. I am afraid I have caused the alang alang to wave, so I close my eyes and lie very, very still, just in case a guard might have noticed. When I finally open my eyes, nothing has changed. I watch for more pieces to drop, and I have lots of time to think. My daydreams are filled with food nowadays.

I remember the delicious treats I bought with my *gobangs* in Madura when Pap served in the Dutch army, the K.N.I.L. I would run to meet him in the driveway when he came home from work, looking so handsome in his uniform. Nothing at all like these Japanese in their ugly khaki, with weapons of punishment hanging from their sides.

"Ah, Ilse," Pap would say. "It has been a hard day." I can almost feel his hand on my shoulder, guiding me toward the verandah where my mother waited, baby Marijke in her arms. I was four years old, and for the first time, a big sister.

"I will need a *piedjit*," he would say.

A back massage! Exactly what I always hoped to hear! I would jump up and down with excitement while Pap hung his shirt over the side of the settee for the babu tjutji to carry off to her washboard. Then he would stretch out, stomach down, on the woven mat that covered our floor, his arms forming a big halo around his head.

My mind also sees Mam sitting in her rattan basket chair. The plumeria blossoms printed on her dress blend in with the lilies printed on the big cushion. In my mind's eye, she looks like she is part of a flower garden and she is the prettiest flower. She would tell Papi about something Marijke did. The baby was very cute. I may have been a little jealous, but I was the older daughter, the one who got to walk up and down Papi's back. I was the only one who could relax the knots, he said. I did not know what a knot was, exactly, but when I stepped on one just right, he roared like a tiger and Mami laughed.

"One gobang for a good job," Pap would say. "Two for an excellent job."

I was never sure what made an excellent job different from a good job. I did my best every time, but hardly ever got two gobangs. But then I was only four years old and one gobang—perhaps two and a half cents—was enough to buy something delicious in the farmers' market, the *Pasar Baru*. Babu Kokki was the only one trusted enough to take me there to spend my gobang.

I would rather go to the Pasar Baru with Babu Kokki than do anything else in the world. Under the roof of a huge pole building, sellers hunker down on their haunches on their *tiekers*–large, colorful braided mats–with their goods piled in the middle. Each tieker has something new and interesting to look at. Everything imaginable is for sale at the Pasar Baru— clothing, handmade toys and decorations, kitchenware and dishes, towels and tablecloths embroidered in fine stitches of every color. And, of course, food. There are dozens of little terra cotta anglos under the roof. The cooks fan the coals with their *kipas* in one hand while they toss ingredients and seasonings into pans and keep them moving with the other. It is a big, noisy place and I try, now, to bring the smell of all that cooking into my nostrils—satay covered with shrimp paste grilled in the *bakkar* method, over the coals; *laos* root that gives our food its special flavor; onions and hot peppers and garlic roasting; sauces made with coconut milk and peanuts. It makes me hurt to remember, but I can't help myself.

Babu Kokki knew all the Javanese who sold the goods they grew or raised or made, and they chattered in their language, *Pasar Maleis*. I could even bargain a little in Pasar Maleis, trying to get as much as I could out of my single gobang. You could get a whole meal for a gobang, but my gobang went for sweet treats. Perhaps *pisang goreng,* the fried bananas that I loved so much. Or better yet, *klepon*—the sweet rice balls which wrapped around a thimbleful of very special palm sugar from Java, the *gula djawa.* The rice was colored green from the *daon pandan* leaf that gave it a special flavor, and then the whole ball was rolled in sweet shredded coconut. So beautiful, and so sweet.

I close my eyes to block out the ugly fence, and I try to block out the noise from the chopping tables so I can concentrate on the taste and the feel of biting into the sugar heart of a klepon. I even take a chance of disturbing the alang alang to raise my imaginary klepon to my lips, and I open my mouth to receive it.

And so I spend my time dreaming of the old days and watching for food in the dirt of the central kitchen, until it is time for me to slide out of the alang alang and go home. I am very excited because I have rescued a cabbage core today. I learned from Babu Kokki that if you plant the core of a cabbage in the soil, it will take root and grow tiny little cabbages that look like brussels sprouts. I can hardly bear to leave this treasure here with the rest of my take for the day, but I will have to wait.

The kitchen workers are scraping off their tables and throwing scraps into the big steel drums. Perhaps a little scraping or two from the chicken or the pork tables will go into the prisoners' pot. They will chip salt from the big block that rests beside the drums in the center of the work area and rub it into those tables to make them clean for tomorrow's work. As they chip the salt with their little axe-like hammers, big splinters fly off and land on the ground, but too far away for me to snag. Too bad. Salt would give the swill some taste.

The guards are very watchful, to make sure no food goes into the pocket of a kitchen worker, and so they are not paying much attention to the fence line. I scoot, inch by inch, down into the ditch and up the other side, my body flat against the ground. Then I watch until I am sure no Japanese is looking my way. When the time is right, I am up on my knees and then on my feet, and I run for home.

After the evening meal, as dusk falls into darkness, I have to find a way to get back to the central kitchen to pick up my prize. With a cabbage core at risk, I can take no chances, so I use my most successful trick for getting away by myself, the one that always works. I have to wait until it is time for the last visit to the squatting holes.

"Come, Ilse," Mam says.

"I don't need to go," I say. I am stretched across my mattress, yawning as if I am ready to go to sleep. She looks at me and I know she is suspicious. "Honestly, Mam. I went after dinner," I lie. "You can leave Edith here." I take Edith and put her on my lap to play with her.

When Mam returns with Marijke and René, I am standing up, bouncing up and down as if I need to go to the toilet.

"I have to go, Mam!" I almost throw Edith at her, to prove I am in a hurry. "Right now," I call over my shoulder, and I am out of the house.

Except for the dim street lights, it is dark, but I know the way. I am lucky tonight—I don't see any guards on the streets.

When I get to the kitchen, I hang back in the shadows until I spot the sentry walking around inside the fence line. I give him time to pass by, and when he is far enough away, I make my move. I run across the street and dive for the ditch. If snakes are there, they will be too startled to do me any harm. I slip into the ditch and stretch out next to my little pile of goodies. Oh, glorious cabbage, I am so happy.

But wait, I must not be careless. I look both ways for the sentry. Sometimes they change directions. I see him across the kitchen yard. He has stopped to light a cigarette. Good. He will take a few minutes to enjoy his smoke. I stuff the cabbage core deep in my pocket and get up on my knees to add the rest. Then I notice the sentry is no longer across the yard. I throw myself back into the ditch, but I am lying on top of the alang alang. I have not had time to wiggle down inside the grass. I don't dare look up to see how close he is, but I feel his boots, thud, thud, thud against the ground. I close my eyes and hold my breath. My teeth are clenched so tight I am afraid they will crack, but I don't make a sound or a movement. Thud, thud, thud, the boots go by. He does not see me. I let out my breath. Thank you, thank you, thank you.

When it is safe to raise my head, I see the guard's back in the distance. I slither back out of the ditch and head for home, my pocket richer than usual.

Mam is glad to see me. She worries when I am out after dark.

"Are you sick, pet?" she asks.

"I don't think so, Mam. Just a little diarrhea." I hope God will not punish me with real diarrhea for lying. "But I have something for you!"

I never break my number one rule: every morsel of food I ever steal or bargain for, I take to Mam for safekeeping and sharing. This time I empty my pockets of everything but the cabbage core. That, I decide, will be a special surprise for Mam, if it grows. Mam takes the rest of it without speaking, as she always does, and then she gives me a long hug, the kind that just wraps me up in her love. As much as she does not want me out foraging for food, she is always grateful for the provisions I bring her.

I never know where she stashes my offerings, and she never knows where I get them. I guess neither of us dares to ask.

Chapter 14.
Gotrik and Lice

I do not remember playing much at Camp Halmaheira. For one thing, I was too busy looking for food. I didn't want to give away my secrets for finding edibles, so I didn't include anyone in my foraging. Hunger motivated me to take chances, but fear motivated me to be cautious. I'm sure I caused Mam a great deal of anxiety with my unexplained absences, but she need not have worried. If I was the daredevil that Mam sometimes called me, then I was the wariest one alive.

Another thing that separated me from others my age was my sense of responsibility. I had crossed a bar when Mam and I vacated that ransacked apartment back at De Hotel. Mam was strong, but how could she protect four children—one but weeks old—by herself? I took on a new role that day, from being a child to being my mother's partner in doing whatever needed to be done.

Playtime was not on the list of necessities, but there were exceptions.

❧

"Get the sheet," I say to Marijke. "I will get the *sisir-sirit*."

It is time for our morning game of Kill the Lice. Oh, how our heads itch with the horrible little vermin that have taken up residence in our hair. My head is De Hotel for head lice, but without the right stuff to kill them and their nit babies, I can't do anything about it. Except play Kill the Lice.

We go outside and spread the piece of white sheeting over a patch of dirt. We get on our knees, across from each other, with the sheet between us. Then we take turns with the sisir-sirit, the special comb with the tiny, fine teeth that chase lice down the hair strands.

"Okay, you go first this time," I say to Marijke, and I hand her the sisir-sirit. She is ready to lower her head and toss her hair forward, and she is giggling. "One—two—three—KILL THE LICE!" I shout.

Her hair flops forward, and she runs the sisir-sirit down a lock of hair, from the scalp forward. Oh, how the evicted lice scurry, but Marijke chases them down and squashes them as fast as she can. She has the fastest thumbs anyone has ever seen in a game of Kill the Lice. Some get away, but she is satisfied with the kill count—nineteen on the first turn. "Did you see when I got three at once?" she brags. That is really a feat in Kill the Lice.

Then it is my turn. My thumbs are not as fast, but I am better at combing them out with the sisir-sirit. "Gotcha!" I shout at one that thought it was going to escape off the edge of the sheet. I get twenty-two, a very good kill for me.

By the time we are finished, the score is eighty-two to seventy-six, Marijke's favor. We are both laughing so hard we have tears. That is the best thing about this game—we can't help but laugh. We play it every morning, and then we help the little ones use the sisir-sirit to chase lice out of their hair.

We still have lice, and we still scratch our heads until they bleed and scab over, and then we scratch off the scabs and they bleed some more. But who knows how much worse it might be if we didn't have our sisir-sirit and if we didn't play Kill the Lice every morning?

I can be beaten at Kill the Lice, but I am definitely the number one champion of the world at *gotrik*, a game that combines baseball and lacrosse. Marijke benefits from my coaching ability, so she is the number two champion. Between us, we can beat everyone in the camp, including the boys. In fairness, the boys are taken off to the work camps when they are ten years old, and I am eleven. So I'm not sure if I could beat a boy my age, or older.

To play gotrik, we have to find a good puck—a sturdy stick, preferably oval and thick, perhaps six to eight inches long and two to three inches wide. Then we have to find good batting sticks, wider at the end if possible, and at least two feet long. Marijke and I are constantly on the lookout for gotrik sticks, as we feel at least half of our success depends upon good equipment. The platform for the puck is always a problem, but today Deitrik has solved it.

"These are perfect!" I am delighted with the bricks our housemate, Deitrik, has brought home. Six of them!

We stack the bricks, edge-on-edge lengthwise, two stacks about five inches apart and maybe ten inches high. The tops are perfectly even. Good. Now I set the puck right across the middle. It makes a little bridge between the stacks. I stand in front of the cross-wise puck, looking down the brick channel. Now, carefully, carefully, I squat, put the point of the bat on the ground under the puck, and then I jerk the bat upward in a swift motion, pulling back just enough to give the puck some backspin. The puck flips up off the bricks, and I give it a good smack—not as good as usual since I am just testing out the set up. It is good. We are ready to play. There are five of us: Deitrik, Marijke, two eight-year-olds from the house next door, and me.

Since Deitrik brought us the bricks—so much better than the uneven rocks we were using before—he gets to go first. He has his cheering section, his brother and sister who are too little to play on our advanced team. "Go, Rikky," they call.

Deitrik concentrates. He plants his batting stick a couple of times, making sure it's in just the right place under the puck. Then he squats and brings the bat up fast. The puck pops straight up, as it should, and as it comes back down, Deitrik gives a mighty swing. That puck would have broken a distance record, only Deitrik missed.

"Oh, too bad, Deitrik," we all say, pretending we are sorry. "That would have been a great hit," we say, glad that it wasn't.

Marijke is next. "May I try a practice swing first?" she asks. "Ilse did."

"Wait a minute, I didn't get to take a practice swing," Deitrik reminds us.

We want to be fair so we decide to start over. But Deitrik and I agree we have already had our practice swings.

Marijke makes a nice practice hit, brings the puck back, and then hits another good one, even farther. This is where she takes off, fast as she can, to where the puck lands. There is no need to run fast, but we always do. Then she begins the measuring process. She picks up the puck and walks it, heel-to-toe, toe-to-heel, all the way back to the bricks, counting as she goes.

"Sixty-nine!" she shouts. That is a good hit, sixty-nine puck-lengths.

Deitrik connects this time and beats Marijke by four puck-lengths. Not bad, but Deitrik is nine, and Marijke is only seven.

Deitrik will have to leave Halmaheira when he turns ten, but it is something we try not to think about. I will tell him Pap's name, just in case Pap is at a work camp and Deitrik goes there. Pap will be glad to know we are all alive. I wish someone could tell us whether Pap is still alive.

The neighbors hit, but one goes off to the side and hits the house. The other one catches the bottom of the puck, and it goes straight up and straight down, six puck-lengths.

Deitrik is ahead. It is up to me. I have had my practice turn, so I am ready. I swing upward. It is a good flip. I haul back my bat and give the puck a solid whack. I beat Deitrik by six puck-lengths. I'm kind of sorry. He brought the bricks. Unfortunately, I break the puck, so now we have to find another one.

I don't know how we found the will or the strength. Malnutrition, dysentery, beriberi, loss of loved ones, despair, fear, pain, humiliation. We experienced all of them, and yet the children played.

Chapter 15.
Women's Work

Besides stocking their own Tea Houses and keeping half-starved women and children under control, the Kempeitai were in charge of general labor recruitment. For women, this included everything from farm work—growing food for the war effort—to prostitution in the infamous brothels maintained for the "comfort" of the Japanese soldiers.

To us, labor recruitment meant being forced to do whatever they demanded, inside or outside our camp. My mother was assigned to a select group that worked outside the gate. She said she worked in the rice fields, but I never, before or after our internment, saw any evidence of rice fields near Camp Halmaheira. It was a mystery never solved. She left the house every day after breakfast to join thirty or forty women at the main gate of the camp. No greetings, no nods or smiles of recognition, nothing to suggest they were comrades in any way. Just a few dozen women trudging in the same direction, eyes downcast.

She left me with two questions to ponder each day, all day: Where does she go? Will she return? Many did not, and we often heard the wailing of those who were left waiting for their mothers or daughters in the evening.

Another day has begun. I let Marijke win the Kill the Lice game. I am watching Mam sitting on the steps of our house, feeding the breakfast bubur dedek to Edith.

I look at Mam's arms. They are skinny, and her shoulders are not as straight as they used to be. Her legs are swollen. They used to be so pretty, so slim and strong when she played tennis with Pap and her friends. I don't think she could play tennis now. She is not eating enough, I know, and I am afraid she has the beriberi that comes when you eat only rice and never get meat or vegetables. I must find a way to make her eat some of the stolen vegetables I bring home from the kitchen. Maybe the cabbage plant will produce its little cabbages soon and there will be enough for all of us.

"Mam, you are so thin. When you go to work, do you get anything to eat?"

"Hush, now, pet. That is nothing for you to worry about," she answers.

But I do worry. What if something happens to Mam? What would we do? The thought is so frightening, I try to put it away from me. Only it sticks in a corner of my mind and keeps me on the edge of a scream most of the time when she is away from the camp.

Mam finishes putting the last bit of porridge into Edith's mouth. She stands up and hands the baby to me. Edith is limp in my arms, and her little eyes stare out at nothing. She used to try to share in her feeding, and her chubby hands would be sticky along with her shirt where she had spread the gruel. And she would be ready for play, her eyes bright and lively. But not now. Her hands are no longer chubby, and her diaper is hardly ever clear of the runny green stuff that means sickness. When she is awake she cries a lot, and then I cuddle her and kiss her forehead and rock her into silence. But sometimes I think I will go crazy if I hear one more "wah" come out of her mouth.

"Marijke, René, come," Mam calls to my sister and brother who have started playing gotrik already. Marijke is teaching René. He's pretty good for only five years old. They are hitting the puck toward the cesspool side of the house. I hope they do not stomp on my cabbage plant.

"To the *mandi bak*," Mam says, and we walk to the cement bathing room on the end of the house. I stand outside and set Edith on the windowless sill. We are not allowed to have a door on the mandi bak or a curtain for the open window. Anyone can look in, and the soldiers often do, but they are not interested today, not in naked little children.

Mam dips the ladle into the water tank and pours water over their bodies. No soap.

We used up the last of it weeks ago, but at least we have plenty of water. I wish I could stand under a shower, but mostly I wish I could have privacy in the mandi bak. I am eleven years old, and privacy has become very important to me.

Marijke and René put on their threadbare coveralls. These will need to be thrown away soon, but not before they begin to fall apart and Mam's magic needle will no longer be able to hold them together. Now for the shoes, all cut out over the toes to give room for their little feet which have gotten bigger. Mine just grew right out over the front of the soles, so I only have shoes up to the balls of my feet, but it gives me a little protection when I go to the squatting holes, and I can point my toes up to keep them out of the muck.

Now comes the time I dread the most. Mam has to leave. She takes off her slendang and puts a new knot, lower down, on the shoulder part. She slips the slendang over my head, as I am now in charge of Edith. She kisses me and blows a kiss toward Edith who is sleeping in my arms.

We all walk together to the street, and then Mam takes Marijke and René across the camp to the orphanage for the day. Marijke and René call it their school, although they would know very little about school, having never been to one. Edith is too sickly to go to with Marijke and René. I'm sorry because I think the children sometimes get a little midday meal there and that would be good for Edith. The Catholic nuns who run the orphanage are the only ones in the camp who are never kicked or beaten. I think the soldiers are very superstitious and are not willing to take any chances with the Catholic God.

I slip Edith into the slendang. She is awake but not crying, for which I am grateful. We go to check on the cabbage. Leaves have begun to grow out of the sides of the core. The under sides of the leaves make me think of armpits, and under those armpits are nubbins which will become little cabbage snacks when they get big enough. I must keep the cabbage from getting too tall and attracting attention. It is swampy by the cesspool, green with grasses, a nice change from the hot, brown dirt of the rest of the camp. It is really very pretty, but no one likes to go there because of the stink. I notice large snails in the grass. They look like the snails that used to crawl up the side of our outdoor sink at home. When there were enough, and when they were big and fat, Babu Kokki would collect them and the servants would have escargot for dinner. But for that, you have to have salt. These snails are big enough and fat enough, but too bad, we have no salt.

Edith and I go to the end of the street, as close to the Kempeitai headquarters as we dare, to catch our last glimpse of Mam for the day. She is in the middle of the group of women headed for the gate, but we spot her when she turns and waves. Then the big gate swings open and she is gone. I try to make my fear go to a place way deep in my insides where it cannot make me shiver all day.

The ladies from our house are very nice about helping me with Edith, so I am free to spend much of the day at the kitchen fence or in those damp places around the camp that might be hiding something to eat, a snake or an edible weed. Always, I am home before the sun begins to sink and the dinner gong sounds, to pick up Edith and return to the edge of the Kempeitai headquarters. The gate swings open, and I hold my breath. One woman after another appears, but my eyes are looking only for my mother. I almost cry with relief when she appears and I am able to breathe again, without fear, until tomorrow morning when she will leave once more. Others are not so lucky, and as Mam takes Edith from my arms, we hear the crying of someone whose mami didn't come home.

There are regular jobs to do around the camp, like helping the nuns, or cooking, or doing the Kempeitai laundry. Why couldn't Mam have gotten one of those easy jobs? Sometimes there are "special" jobs, and those are never easy. Women must do the dirtiest work in this camp, and the most difficult. Sometimes they do not survive, the work is so hard. The guards pick women for these special duties at the morning roll call.

The guard stops in front of Mam. "Omae," he grunts, and points down the street where some other women are gathering. "*Asoko he ike. Isoge. Hoka ni shigoto ga aru.*"

"You—go—hurry up—there is another job to be done," he is saying.

Mam hands Edith and the slendang to me. "Take René and Marijke to the nuns," she says, and she is off before the guard gets impatient enough to slap or kick her. She is wearing one of her pretty dresses, the pale moss green one with a design of bamboo stalks and leaves. It is one of the few things she has left from the pillowcase wardrobe. Her hair is pinned high on her head. I think she looks more beautiful than usual, even though she is stick-thin down to her ankles which are beginning to look like sand dunes overflowing her stretched-out sandals. She is stronger than most, though, and she still moves quickly.

I herd the children through the breakfast line and rush them through their bowls of porridge. Edith whimpers as I shove bubur gedek into her little mouth, not bothering to fish out even the biggest of the brown husks. I must be done with the morning duties so I can find out where Mam is working.

Mrs. Goettje comes to the step and takes Edith from my lap. "Go on, my dear," she says. She is one of the nice ones. She understands I am worried about Mam.

No time to bother with face-washing, so Marijke and René still have rice mush in the corners of their mouths when I take them through the gate into the courtyard of the orphanage. They are both panting for breath; we have run all the way, through the streets of the camp. René plops down on his rear and starts to cry, but I turn my back on him and run back out the gate. Out of the corner of my eye, I see one of the sisters walking toward him. He will be okay; I want to find Mam.

I head first to the toilets because I need to go. It is worse than ever because most of the holes have filled up. The smell is so disgusting I pull the front of my dress up over my nose, and I can smell my own body warmth and sweat which is a lot better than the stink hole I am squatting over. We have been in Camp Halmaheira for a year now, but I am still ashamed when the guard walks by. At least he is at a far distance. I suppose he does not want to be too near this stinking place.

As soon as I can get away from the squatting hole, I see a lady who goes to work with Mam every morning. She, too, must have been chosen to stay in camp today. She is carrying an empty square can by its bale, a bucket that used to have lard in it. Lots of lard—it is a huge bucket. I recognize it from the central kitchen. She is walking away from the toilet area, so I run to catch up with her and tap her on the back of her shoulder. She turns to look at me. Her eyes are sunk deep in her head, and I can see she is sick. I look downward and I see that her hands are covered with dirt.

"Please," I say to her. "Do you know where my mother is? Mies—Maria Christina Evelijn Veere. You go to work with her every morning."

The woman's eyes smile at me, but it's like her mouth doesn't have enough energy to smile too. "Yes, girl, I know where she is. Follow me."

We walk a few blocks to an area near the fence where there are no houses. My mother is at the head of a line of women. They seem to be digging a long hole. Mam is loosening up the dirt with a *patjol*—a hoe—and the others are coming along behind to scoop the dirt into their lard buckets. There are three lines, all doing the same thing. This is going to be a very big hole. The dirt is hard-packed, from the heat I suppose, and it is not easy to loosen. I bend down and pick up a dry clod.

Mam's hair is already falling down, and her dress is all smeared with dirt. She is not happy to see me. "Ilse, what are you doing here?" she whispers, and her voice hisses. "Are the children all right?"

"Mam, I just wanted to know where you went," I begin.

"Get out of here. Right now. Before they put you to work, too." Mam pushes some loose hair off her sweaty forehead, and she leaves a streak of dirt.

"What are you doing? Why are you digging a hole?"

Mam stops hoeing and stands in front of me. Her face twists in a strange way, and she takes my shoulders and shakes me once. Hard. Her hands are strong.

"Ilse, if you have never done as I say before, you must do it now. Get away from this place and don't ask questions." She pushes me so hard I almost fall down, but I stay on my feet and stagger backwards. Then I turn so she cannot see my tears, and I run toward home. But as soon as I am out of her sight, I stop and wipe my tears with my hands. Now I have dirt smears on my face, too, like Mam, and I want to go back and help her dig the hole. Instead, I hide behind the corner of a house where I can watch.

It is so hot, but the women are not given any time to rest. One lady faints—the one who took me to my mother. A soldier kicks her, and she rolls over, but she cannot get up and go back to work. In a few minutes, another woman shows up to take her place. I think if I had stayed, the soldiers would have thought me old enough, at eleven and a half, to dig. I want to take some water to the women, but I am afraid of what my mother might do and even more afraid of what the soldiers might do.

I go home to tend to Edith, but I slip back to my hiding place from time to time.

The hole gets longer and deeper, until someone brings a ladder to get in and out of it. The cans of dirt are now pulled up by a rope and emptied onto a patch of bare ground. They become small mountains of dirt, and I think René might like to play there. But why are they digging this enormous hole in the ground? It is time to go for Marijke and René. I don't know when they will let Mam come home. I have found no food today. It will be a hungry night.

Mam comes home at the sound of the dinner gong, but she is too tired to go to the central kitchen. Her dress is filthy and so is she. She goes straight to the mandi bak, and I take the children to the central kitchen. I take her bowl along just in case they will fill it, but they don't. When we return, Mam is asleep. I put half of my dinner into her bowl and set it and Edith's red pepper on the window sill for her to find if she wakes in the night. Then I help the little ones prepare for bed. The squatting holes are too awful, so I take Marijke and René out to the cesspool, then to the mandi bak, and finally to bed and prayers.

When Mam wakes with the rest of us at the morning gong, she looks very happy to see the leftover dinner on the window sill. She takes a few sips of the broth.

"My darling, you are so good to take care of your mami." Then she divides the rest among our bowls. "A little bonus for breakfast," she says.

I need to talk to Mam. I am still stinging over what happened yesterday.

"Why did you push me away, Mam? And why couldn't I help?"

"I do not want you there, Ilse. Is that not clear?"

"But why, Mam? Why can't I help? And why do you have to dig such a big hole, anyway?"

Mam closes her eyes and takes in a long breath. I know she thinks I am being stubborn and disobedient.

"My love," she explains, "the toilets must be emptied. The hole is where the filth from the squatting holes will go."

"But who is going to take the filth—" Oh no, what I am thinking cannot be true. Surely my mother will not have to—"Do not try to come to me today, Ilse. Stay as far away as you can."

I understand, but I do not want to believe it.

When breakfast is over, Mam goes off to the squatting holes to finish the job. As soon as I can, I go to see what is happening, but I keep my distance. She and the other women are using smaller cans to dip the sick filth into the large square lard buckets. When the guards decide the work is not going fast enough, some of the women have to use their bare hands.

It looks like the lard buckets are too heavy to carry when they are full, so the women fill them only halfway. But this is not fast enough for the guards. One of them disappears and brings back a long thick pole. He hands it to Mam and barks some orders at her.

Mam and another woman fill up one of the big buckets to the brim. They put the pole through the bucket's bale. Then they shoulder the pole, one on each end, to carry the full can to the big hole. I can see tears pouring down my mother's face. Or perhaps it is sweat, in the blistering heat. She has a handkerchief tied over her nose. The can sloshes over as they walk. Poor Mam has to walk through the mess because she is at the back of the pole. Then suddenly the pole snaps and my mother is covered in the contents of the bucket.

The guard kicks each of them once in the stomach and points to the mess on the ground. I watch while they try to clean up the mess with water and a broom, but it is hopeless. I leave to see if I can find some soap or disinfectant, but I can't. When I return, they are all back to filling the buckets half full.

How many ladles of water from the mandi bak will it take to clean my mother's body tonight, and her gentle soul?

Chapter 16.
Snail Soup

The Kempeitai were masters at regulating the fine line between starvation and malnutrition. We were all suffering from malnutrition—some more severely than others. At the time I would have said we were all starving. Not that it matters much, for chronic malnutrition leads to death, too.

In children, severe malnutrition slows growth, causes weakness and lethargy and eventually leads to total loss of appetite and difficulty in swallowing. These are danger signs, and Edith had them all. She was over a year old, but she lay, listless, showing no sign of wanting to stand or move about, or even to sit up on her own. She stopped crying and gave up eating. All she swallowed was water, and precious little of that. Mam was frantic, and I remember crying myself to sleep every night.

One of the prisoners was a Dutch doctor. She was sympathetic, but honest.

"Your little girl is dying. She must have protein. It is her only hope. Soon she will stop swallowing altogether, and then she will be gone."

And where are we to get protein? I search desperately for a garden snake or a rodent, but I can't even find grubs. Everyone is looking for such things now. I keep thinking about the fat snails out by the cesspool swamp. They would make a rich broth if only I could get them out of their shells and de-slime them. I know exactly how to go about it; I watched Babu Kokki do it dozens of times. But I need salt.

From the ditch outside the central kitchen, I stare at the huge salt blocks resting in the middle of the cooking area. The cooks hack off chunks of the precious stuff and grind it up to season the food. Bits and pieces fly off and come to rest on the ground, but too far away for me to retrieve. A plan begins to form in my mind. Oh, it is so risky, but my little sister's life depends upon it.

It is bedtime; Mam is busy with Edith, getting her to swallow water out of a thimble. Finally she gives up and just wets her finger and sticks it in Edith's mouth.

I sit up straight on my mattress as if I have a sudden pang in my gut.

"Oh! I have to go," I announce, and I scramble onto my feet.

"Ilse, wait. I'm almost finished..." Mam does not want me to go out so late, alone.

"No, no!" I tell her. "I have to go right now." And I am out the door, on my way to the central kitchen. It is quite dark, but I can see my way. I am careful to avoid any guards that might be on patrol.

I slip into the ditch and take my place next to the fence, as close to the big cooking drums as I can get. There is a dim yard light flickering near the drums, and I can see the square salt blocks nearby. They are nearly as tall as my shoulder. From here I can see the ground littered with small slivers of salt, and that is what I am after. But I must wait for total darkness. For some reason, there is no guard tonight. Or if there is, it is a Javanese and he is having a nap somewhere. I must be silent. I am very good at being silent—I have had lots of practice.

Soon it is dark enough for me to test the ground, and I find a place that dips, deepening the space between the ground and the lowest strand of barbed wire. With my bare hands I scrape away the earth on both sides of the wire, to make a hole for my body to slide under. I lie on my back, press myself against the dirt, and begin to slither, like a snake, under the wire. I can lift it just enough to get my highest part—my head—under, and then I slide, slide, slide, working my shoulders and my heels together to keep moving. It is taking so long, and I expect to hear boot steps or shouting any second. My heart pounds so hard it hurts.

At last, I am all the way under the fence. I am in the central kitchen. I stay low and scoot along the shadows. Embers still burn under the cooking drums, and I know now how I am going to cook my broth. But first, the salt.

My coveralls have a large patch pocket, and I have brought handkerchiefs. I work in the shadow behind the salt blocks where I am hidden from sight. It takes only seconds to scoop up enough salt to fill the pocket, and I stuff the handkerchiefs in on top of it. I would not want to lose the prize after I have gotten this far. I stand and run, fast, under the shadows that surround the circle of light, and on to the fence. Again, I slide under the barbed wire and back down into the ditch. This time it seems to take no time at all.

I am feeling very confident, so I stand up to make sure the handkerchiefs have held and the salt is safe. But wait, I hear the sound of boots, walking up the street. I drop into the grass and freeze. I do not breathe until I hear the sentry pass by. He does not know I am here. When I dare to look, he is far away. I jump out of the ditch and run as fast as I can in the opposite direction. It is the long way home, and I have already been gone too long.

When I get back to my mattress, Mam is crying, and she is very, very angry.

"Ilse," she says when she is able to talk. "You were not at the squatting holes. I went after you, and no one had seen you."

I wanted it to be a surprise, but I show her my pocketful of salt. "I need it for the snails," I explain, but I am not sure she understands. After all, she is not the one who spent all those hours with the babu kokki. I do not dare to tell her my whole plan, for she would put a stop to it before it even got started.

The next morning before roll call, I find the big snails, as usual, in the grass. I pull them off the grass and remove the bits of bark and wood that stick to them. I turn each one upside down and pour ground-up salt into its flesh. Slime bubbles up and oozes over the sides of the shell, and soon the snail shrivels so that I can shoe-horn it out with my thumbnail. Fifteen fat snails come out of their shells. No slime. They go into an old Quaker Oats can I found a long time ago. I cover them with water, and then I hide the can in the tall grass near the stinking cesspool, trusting that no one will come near the stench.

I spend the day carrying out the rest of my plan. With a rusty nail and a rock as a hammer, I punch two holes in the Quaker Oats can. Then I search the camp until I find a piece of old clothesline wire. I fasten that to the holes to form a wire bale for the can. I will use my gotrik stick to pick the can up by the bale and set it on the hot coals under one of the cooking drums. I plan to hide while the water boils, and then I will remove the can in the same manner. At last I am ready. All I need is nightfall.

Mam knows I'm up to something when I get up from my mattress and pick up my gotrik stick.

"I suppose you have a great need to use the toilet," she says. Her eyes squint and she bites her lower lip.

I don't know what to say. I decide to tell the truth, but not all of it.

"Well, I have something that I need to do. But don't worry about me."

Mam stares at me and I stare back. It seems like a long time, but I have the feeling we have come to an understanding. She will not ask me what I need to do and then I will not have to lie. I leave without saying more.

I go to the cesspool to retrieve my snails and then to the mandi bak to fill the Quaker Oats can with fresh water. At last, I am off again for the central kitchen.

It works exactly as I have planned. The water boils while I lie hidden in the shadows. The sentry doesn't suspect a thing, and what luck—he disappears when it is time to remove the can from the embers, and he doesn't come back.

When I return home, very late, I have snail broth full of protein for Edith. Mam, Marijke, René and I feast on snails. With salt.

Chapter 17.
Christmas 1944

Looking back, I can take stock of our blessings at the end of 1944. We were all alive, a lucky family. Edith was still weak, but at eighteen months old she was toddling and had a mind of her own which often gave us the gift of laughter.

After a year and a half of imprisonment, a house furnished with wall-to-wall mattresses—no furniture at all—seemed normal. We had three oversized cot mattresses—thick mats, really—stuffed with kapok, not the fluffy kind of batting that holds it shape, but the cheap kind that flattens down and gets hard. My mother and I pushed our two together, and Edith slept between us. The third stretched across the bottom ends of our two mattresses, and Marijke and René slept toe-to-toe on it. This mat carpet took up the corner of the room, with a narrow footpath around the outer edges, a miniature brand-gang between us and the other families that occupied the room. Our belongings, pitiful few that they were, fit neatly in the space between the mattresses and the wall, and the wide sill of the tall window served as a shelf. Luxury quarters, in that place.

I suppose we made friends in camp, but I do not remember socializing being part of camp life. In truth, we were too busy trying to survive, and our own family was the core of our society.

Besides, friends "get together," and that was against the rules. Social event or coup attempt, the punishment was harsh.

As the kapala kongsie, Mam held fast to the rule forbidding kumpulans. With one exception: December 24, 1944.

It is Christmas Eve and I am hunting bedbugs. My mattress makes me think of hills and valleys. It has lines of stitching from top to bottom, about four inches apart. They make the valleys. The worn out old kapok is supposed to puff up on both sides of the lines of stitching. Those are the hills, but they are smashed down over the stitching, hiding the valleys. I have made a wonderful discovery. The bedbugs like to burrow down into the valleys. They think they are safe there, but I outsmart them. With my thumbs flat, one on either side of the stitched line, I spread apart the kapok and open up the valley.

Aha! I can catch whole families, but I have to be fast because they run in all directions to find another valley to hide in. I squeeze them and crush them between my fingernails, and the blood they gorged themselves on the night before squirts out. When I am finished with the kill, I have blood all over my fingers and more bloodstains on my mat, and a strong smell, very much like almonds, rises up. I don't care. I'm glad they are dead, and when I am finished with one valley, I go on to another one to drive out more bedbug families.

I know it makes little difference in the bedbug population, but at least I feel less helpless. And it is something to do. But the light from the ceiling is too dim, so I stop.

The house is very quiet tonight. Unusual. Maybe everyone is thinking about their Christmases back before the war. I hear

René scratching again. Scratching makes it worse, but he won't listen, so I don't bother to tell him any more. I think Edith is sleeping, but it's hard to tell. Anyway, she isn't crying. Mam and Marijke have gone to bathe in the mandi bak. Now I hear them coming through the house, down the paths between the mattresses.

"Merry Christmas, Maria," I hear from several women, and Mam whispers the same to them.

When she gets back to our space, Marijke goes to her mattress and flops down. Mam turns out the light. I think she is going to hear the little ones whisper their prayers as usual. I am old enough to say my own prayers without supervision. I always ask for food, and I ask God to keep us alive. He does not do so well at giving us this day our daily bread, but we are all alive, and I can thank him for that. Of course I do not know about Pap. He is so far away in my memory.

Tonight I will thank God for the Baby Jesus. The manger was no better than this house, but at least Jesus had shepherds and angels who worshipped him instead of guards who hated him. I hope the hay was clean and it didn't have biting bugs in it.

But Mam is not getting ready to hear prayers. Instead, she scootches on her knees across the ends of our mattresses to the window sill. Whatever is she doing? She digs down into one of the old pillowcases and brings out a white candle stuck into a holder that used to be a tin can. All four of us sit up to watch her scootch back and set the candle in the pathway beside her mattress. Then, wonder of wonders, she pulls a book of matches out of her pocket and lights the candle.

"Oh, Mam!" I say. It just bursts right out of me, and I hear "ooh!" and "aah!" bursting right out of other people, too.

Mam's face is beautiful in the candlelight, and her eyes are soft with a smile. She reaches under her pillow and pulls out her tiny Bible with the leather cover. Then she sits back and pats the mattress beside her. My sisters and my brother and I crawl across our mattresses to get close to her. She opens her Bible to the second chapter of the Gospel of Luke and begins to read the Christmas story by the light of the candle.

"And it came to pass in those days, that there went out a decree from Caesar Augustus, that all the world should be taxed..."

I am sure that Mam means this little celebration to be for us, her children only, but one by one, everyone in the household creeps into our candle-lit room to hear the blessed words. Every person in the house is present. It is a kumpulan, but Mam does not stop to make them all go back to their own mattresses. In the light from the street lamp, we see a Japanese guard walking toward our window. Mam does not see him, for she is reading.

"For unto you is born this day in the city of David..."

He peers into the window, and does a double take at what he sees by the light of our candle.

"...a saviour..." No one moves.

"...which is Christ the Lord."

"Aaaaaah-hah!" he says, in a voice that starts low and then rises. "*Sore-ha nanda?*" he yells. What is that?

Everyone in the room is perfectly still. Mam does not move a muscle. We must look like one of those dioramas we used to make in school, to show some kind of history scene.

Another soldier comes to the window, and they both look in at us. One grunts something to the other, and as suddenly as they came, they leave. No more yelling, no threats. They just turn around and walk away. You can hear everyone start breathing again.

Mam finishes the story, and one of the ladies starts to sing "Silent Night." We all join in, keeping our voices low.

"Stille nacht, heilige nacht, alles slaapt, sluimert zacht…"

It sounds so beautiful, I want it to go on forever. We do not have the comforting presence of the stable animals, nor the adoration of shepherds. But we have each other and the light of the candle. And angels must, surely, have been protecting us when the guards appeared at the window.

When the song is over, Mam blows out the candle and everyone goes to bed. We go to sleep, still huddled close to Mam.

Chapter 18.
The Tomato

War news was not available to us in Camp Halmaheira. Had it been, we would have taken heart in knowing that by the early months of 1945 Japan was struggling. All we knew was that camp conditions worsened. Newcomers poured into Camp Halmaheira from other camps, and the houses became more crowded than ever.

The newcomers came with little but the rags they wore. Those of us who had arrived with sufficient clothing had outgrown it or watched it disintegrate. The Japanese started stacking gunnysacks in the common areas. Most of them displayed the word for rice—"*rijst*" in Dutch or "*beras*" in Maleis. Some had pictures of rice fields. I sorted down through the stacks to find the softest, most attractive ones and took them home to turn into shifts for us to wear—an easy job for Mam, with her ever-present needle and thread. Scooped-out neck, slitted armholes and a rope around the waist transformed a gunnysack into camp wear.

Every day the *grobak*, pulled by a lumbering water buffalo, rumbled to the main gate, its flat bed stacked with the day's-worth of bodies rolled up in bamboo mats. The feet of dead adults stuck out beyond the ends of the rolls, flopping up and down as the wagon bumped along. The feet of little children stayed put, deep inside their rolls. Loved ones who could still walk followed behind, weeping and lamenting if they had strength to use their voices. They stopped at the gate, and the wagon went on with its cargo of tubular dead, to some unknown burying place. Halmaheira was populated by the dying and the near-dying, it seemed.

Supplies of edibles were drying up, with ever more people foraging. Snakes were a delicacy, and pity the poor cat that might try to pussyfoot through. I learned that hunger is painful. When the digestive acids have no food to dissolve, they turn on the digestive organs themselves. The little ones cried with pain, and I was torn between wanting to slap them into silence and wanting to cry myself—for their agony as well as my own. I made regular raids on the central kitchen, and when I couldn't find food, I brought back salt and charcoal—salt for the gastropods and grasshoppers we ate, and charcoal to slow down the effects of dysentery. And occasionally, a vegetable.

Only once was I caught.

I cannot believe my good luck. A whole tomato! It is perfect—round, as big as my fist, and red, like only a fresh, ripe tomato can be. It was right next to the barbed wire—I had only to lift the bottom strand and pull it to me. Now that I have it in my hand, I just have to lie on my stomach in the alang alang for a few minutes to look at it. A tomato! Mam once traded away a very fancy set of sheets for some red tomatoes. Oh, they were so good!

I close my eyes and imagine how it will feel when I bite into my beautiful tomato—my front teeth will come together to puncture the outer skin and then sink through the fleshy part. I will suck the acidy juice from the pocket I have opened up, careful not to lose a drop of it or a single seed, in my imaginary feast. It won't be imaginary for long—I will take it home and tonight, when Mam is home, we will all have our bites of tomato. REAL bites.

I open my eyes again, to look at my tomato. But I am not seeing only the tomato. I am also seeing a very shiny steel toe of a boot and the point of a sword. Maybe if I don't look up, the boot and the sword will pass by. I finger the sharp edges of the grass, and I can feel the sweat trickle down my neck. Please go away, I pray, please, please, please. But that does not happen.

The boot moves forward and nudges my shoulder.

"Tate!" Get up.

I get to my knees, and then to my feet, but I don't look up. I bow low, as low as I can without revealing the tomato I have in my right hand, behind my back.

"Naore!" Stand up straight.

I do, but I keep my hand behind my back. The sword taps my right shoulder.

"Sore-ha nanda?" What is that?

I do not answer. I see that he is holding his hand out, palm up. I do not budge.

The sword again taps my right shoulder, not so easy this time.

"Dase!" Give it to me.

My mind is trying to tell me I could be beaten, or burned, or hung upside down, but all I can think about is my beautiful tomato, and I cannot hand it over to Takahase. He is the officer we are most afraid of.

I look up at him. I think of my Papi on his horse, and I give Takahase a terrible frown. I am so scared, but I do not hand over the tomato.

Takahase sucks in his breath through his clenched teeth. This is a very bad sign. When he steps toward me, I bring my hand to my mouth like lightning and take a huge bite out of my tomato. Then I throw it off to the side and take off running. I am not fast enough. The steel boot catches me on the shinbone. I see bursts of light from the pain, but I keep on running, and I do not stop until I get to my mat, bleeding, and crying because it hurts so bad and because I have lost the most beautiful tomato in the world.

My craving for tomatoes never went away. Nor did the boot print scar on my left shin. I suppose I should have considered myself lucky that I was not the center of a public punishment that day. I stole food and defied a high-ranking Kempeitai officer. Months of a festering, painful wound was small price to pay for such satisfaction, but I wished I had been just a little bit faster.

Chapter 19.
The Arrest

May, 1945. Edith had turned two, a little girl. I turned twelve, officially a young lady, but in truth I had relinquished my childhood long before. I began to listen to the forbidden political news that filtered into camp with new prisoners.

Hope is at a premium in a place like Camp Halmaheira. Mostly you hope you will find something to eat today that will quiet the constant gnawing in your gut. But hanging above your survival-level hope is the remote hope that someone stronger than your oppressors will show up and liberate you. You hope that the big gate will open and you can go home—maybe not the one you left, but another like the one you remember.

So news about the Allies on the move against Japan gave hope of liberation a fluttering chance. But we also heard news of young native islanders—*pemudas*—shouting *merdeka*—freedom—and beheading Hollanders and Indies alike. How could this be? These were the people of my babu kokki, the people of the Pasar Baru where I spent my gobangs. Where was home? Camp Halmaheira? Never! Outside these walls? Not if someone out there wanted to cut off my head.

Imagine my anguish. Everywhere I looked inside the camp, more death—from beatings, from malnutrition, from disease. But it was apparently no better for us outside the camp. How could it get any worse?

I was about to find out.

❧

Mrs. H. is a troublemaker. I have never trusted her. She is whining to my mother about wanting to have a card party.

"Be reasonable, Maria. We can put the children to bed, and after they are asleep, we can hide behind the wall in Katrin's room." It is the one place in the house not in direct view of a window or a door. "What can it hurt?"

"It is forbidden, Grethe. It will hurt plenty when you are caught and they set fire to the matches driven under your fingernails."

I cringe, and so does Mrs. H. That is the most recent torture we have witnessed, of a new prisoner who met with a group—a kumpulan—to share news of the outside world. Her shrieks are still in my ears.

"But that was political," she says. "We only want to have some fun. We deserve it."

"Politics—fun—the Kempeitai don't care, Grethe. It is all a kumpulan to them. We will not give them reason to come into this house and beat us. I said no. There will be no more talk of card parties."

My mother is a strong woman, and I am proud of the way she stands up to Mrs. H.

Mrs. H. slinks back to her family. I hear whispering. She is always trying to break the rules, and she always thinks she knows best.

Mam smiles at me and shakes her head. We know what the other is thinking, Mam and I. We are that close.

"Ilse, I will take the children to the toilet tonight. Would you like to have some time to yourself?"

I nod. Tonight Marijke can help Edith squat without falling or getting her hands in the mess. I can use the time in the mandi bak. I gather up my bathing materials as Mam gathers up the children.

Hurray! The mandi bak has no line, and there is no sign of a Japanese guard. I can pour as many ladles of water over myself as I wish. I strip off my shift, ragged thing that it is, when I see movement out the window. Oh, no! I grab my shift to hold it over my breasts, and I turn to see a soldier. But he is walking away from me, and looking into the house. I lean out the empty window frame of the mandi bak.

The light is on in Katrin's area, and I hear women's voices, cackling and ooh-ing and ah-ing. My stomach lurches. Mrs. H. has taken advantage of my mother's absence to start her card party. Then I hear a lot of shouting, and soldiers come running from all directions.

I am trying to put my clothes back on, but my hands are shaking. By the time I get back into my shift, the guards are storming the house. I hear their billy clubs landing on flesh, and I am grateful that my family is not there. I can see the women being driven out of the house. Soldiers are kicking, swinging their Samurai swords and their billy clubs, shouting at the women to stand up while they beat them down, and to run while they club them to a standstill. Children are screaming; their mothers are bleeding. This is the worst thing that has ever happened in our house, and then I see why. One of the Japanese officers is kicking Mrs. H. who has fallen to the ground. His teeth are clenched in a snarl as his boots land their blows. In his fist he is holding tarot cards.

Mrs. H.'s card party was a tarot reading. It is one of the most forbidden of all things at Camp Halmaheira, to predict the future. I break and run for the squatting holes, to warn Mam and the children. I meet them a few blocks from home.

"Mam, Mam," I sob, unable to get my breath. "You must not go home!" I tell her in gasping spurts what has happened. I know they will blame her because she is the kapala kongsie.

"Don't worry, Ilse. I was not home, therefore I could not have prevented it."

"Oh, Mam, they will blame you anyway—'When one is guilty, all are guilty'—please do not go home." I pull on her arm, I am desperate, but she keeps telling me not to worry.

So we go home, and a soldier is waiting for her. I turn my pleading to him.

"Oh, please, *gunjin-san*, my mother hasn't done anything wrong. Please let her stay home." I am crying so hard, tears and snot stream down my face. The soldier looks disgusted and turns away.

Mam kisses me. "Don't worry, my darling. I will be back soon."

She nods to the soldier, and they walk off down the street. The soldier pushes her with his sword and tells her to walk faster. I leave the children crying on the doorstep and follow my mother at a distance. When she gets to the Kempeitai head-quarters I see the other women from our house lined up outside the building they use for the camp jail. I hide behind a tree, and I hear the soldiers yelling.

All of a sudden one soldier pushes Mam to the ground and hits her with the broad side of his sword and yells, "Are you guilty?"

Mam gets up, proud, and says, "No, I am not guilty because I was not home and therefore could not have prevented it."

The guard makes her kneel and he beats her again and again, but her answer is always, "Not guilty."

I am shaking, and then I realize Marijke is beside me, also shaking. I wrap my arms around my little sister, and we hold each other as we watch how they torture Mam. God, make them stop! Please, God, we pray.

When the sword goes up one more time to hit Mam, my sister screams and instantly the search lights are on us.

Mam turns her head and sees us. Then she says, "Yes, I am guilty," and collapses to the ground.

The guard raises his sword and yells, "Satu salah, semuah salah!"

When one is guilty, all are guilty. The soldiers take Mam and the other women into the Kempeitai jail. Marijke and I go home where we cry for our mother and beg God to return her to us.

Chapter 20.
The Handkerchief

Somehow we got through that night. I don't know how the other motherless children in the house fared. I only remember that René, Edith, Marijke and I huddled together across the place where Mam should have been, and we cried and we prayed and perhaps we slept. Fear and grief are exhausting.

I am trying to do things as Mam would be doing them. I am in charge now.

"Hush, hush, my darling *schatjes*," I tell the little ones when they start to cry. "Mami will be home soon." But I am crying, too.

The morning roll call in front of our house is only children. The guard does not even bother to stop. We go to the central kitchen for our morning porridge. After breakfast I send Marijke and René to the mandi bak to clean up, and then I give them clean clothes for the day. I feel like a machine, going through motions. Every second, I am watching for the women of our house to come up the street. It is time to deliver Marijke and René to the nuns. I tell them not to worry, Mam will be home when they return tonight.

Please, God, please, please, please, I pray all the way home, Edith toddling along beside me. But no women have returned.

I sit on the front steps with my little sister in my lap, and at last I see women from our house coming up the street. One by one they walk by me, and I see how badly they have been beaten, their faces swollen, lips split, and teeth missing. I look frantically for my mother. But she does not come home. My tears will not stop. When I ask the other women what has happened to her, they cannot tell me because they do not know. Mrs. H. has returned, but I do not speak to her. I will never speak to her.

All I can do is cry and pray for Mam. And hope upon hope that I will look down that street and see her walking toward me—broken, toothless, bloody—I will take care of her whatever they have done to her. I want my Mami. I need her. I love her. But the day passes into night, and we wait, still.

The next morning, as we are eating our breakfasts, a guard comes to the house.

"Where is the daughter of Maria Christina Evelijn Veere?" he asks, not shouting.

I stand up. My voice is stuck in my throat and I am shaking in fear of what I am going to hear. If it were good news, Mam would be here herself.

"Your mother is being jailed in the Kempeitai headquarters."

My voice comes unstuck in a blast of words. "But why? She did not do anything wrong. Why isn't the woman who had the tarot cards in jail? This woman, right here," and I point to Mrs. H. I expect to be kicked, but I don't care.

The soldier shrugs. "I have told you what you need to know," he says and he leaves. No kick.

Inside myself I am screaming: This is not right! It is unfair! My mother did not do anything wrong! She has been a good kapala kongsie! She always makes the women abide by the rules! We need her here, with us. I cannot go on by myself.

It comes to me, what I must do, but I am so terrified at the very thought, I think I may throw up.

I do not take Marijke and René to the nuns. I clean up Edith and dress her in a little jumpsuit that Marijke wore when we first arrived in this place. I put gunnysack shifts on René and Marijke, and I put on one of my mother's shifts with flowers on it, one that I remember from our days in Medan. It is too big, but I am dressing up for this occasion, just like church. I wonder if it might be Sunday. Then I pick up Edith, and we all go to the end of the street and head up the low hill to the main building of the Kempeitai headquarters. I have never been this close.

It is all I can do to make myself climb the steps to the wide porch. The only thing that keeps me from backtracking is that they have my mother and I must get her back. I push René and Marijke ahead of me, and I hitch Edith higher on my hip. René is so scared, he shakes all over.

I push open the wide door, and we step over the threshold. I see a large room, with four soldiers standing by a pillar. They seem to be visiting. One sees us and walks over.

"What do you want?" he asks in Maleis that sounds more like Japanese.

"I have come to get my mother, Maria Christina Evelijn Veere. Can you tell me where she is?" My voice is wobbly and high, but I speak loud enough.

The soldier frowns, not a mean frown. "Wait here," he says, and he disappears into a room that opens onto this large foyer.

The little ones cling to me. Edith is getting heavy in my arms, but I don't dare put her down. We wait for a long time, and finally, an officer comes out of the room. I am glad it is not Takahase. He might have remembered the tomato incident. We all bow, low. It is very important to show our respect right now.

"You are the children of Mrs. Evelijn Veere?" he asks. I am glad that he speaks much better Maleis than the last one.

"Yes, *shookoo-san*," I say, remembering the word for "officer." Then I blurt it all out. "My mother has been a good kapala kongsie, shookoo-san. She has always made sure everyone abides by the rules. She was not home when Mrs. H. brought out the tarot cards. My mother would never have permitted it. Please, shookoo-san, we need our mother. This baby needs her mother. We cannot get along without her. My mother has done nothing wrong."

René begins to sob. Marijke and I break into tears, too. Our lives are in this Kempeitai officer's hands, and I know that Mam, the little ones, and I are nothing to him. We are probably bedbugs in the valley as far as he is concerned, and he wouldn't mind exterminating us on the spot.

I am surprised. I think I see a little sympathy in his eyes, and I am hopeful that our tears have softened his heart enough to let my mother go.

He squats to speak with René. "Little boy," he says, "I cannot let your mother go."

My heart drops.

The officer stands back up to speak to me. "Your mother has committed a very serious crime, and she has not been cooperative."

"But, shookoo-san," I begin, and stop when he shakes his head.

"She cannot go home with you. She has been put into solitary confinement."

My mouth drops open, and I gasp. My heart tightens up, my head swims, and I think I may stop breathing and fall to the floor. Solitary confinement? Those terrible little huts that stand in the sun behind the headquarters building? Where women go and do not come home, or if they do come home, they die soon after?

The officer puts his arm out, ready to catch me if I fall, but I do not fall. Instead, I hug Edith closer, but I cannot stop the tears. And I cannot help but whisper, "Why?" It is Mrs. H. who should be in solitary confinement, for what she has done to my mother. Oh, how I hate Mrs. H.

The officer does not answer my question, but he takes my arm and leads me out of the headquarters. Marijke and René follow along behind us. We all walk down the steps and around the building where the solitary confinement cells are lined up. Four, maybe five. They are tiny, like the telephone booths on city street corners, but smaller. I think Mam can stand up, but I am sure there is no room to lie down.

The cells are not shaded. They must be like anglos, steaming human flesh. The officer points to one, and I cannot bear to think that my mother is there, inside. I begin to sob again, great loud sobs and I hope Mam cannot hear me. The little ones cry, too, even though I don't think they understand what is happening to our mother. Maybe Marijke does.

The officer actually looks at me, and I can see he does not mean me harm.

"The only thing I can do is give you permission to come to your mother's cell each day and bring clean clothes to her."

It is enough to give me a little boost of hope. I put Edith down on the ground and pull the loose bodice of Mam's dress up over my face, to dry the tears.

"I can see her every day?"

"Yes, but you may not speak to her." His eyes turn hard, to show he means business. "You may not smile or cry or communicate with her in any way. She is in solitary confinement."

I have been blown apart by something worse than a bomb. I cannot even talk with my own mother? All I can do is walk by like a robot, deliver the clean clothes, pick up the dirty ones, and leave?

"Be glad you can take clean clothes to her," he says. I think he has read my mind. "If you do more—if you try to communicate with her or smuggle anything to her, she will be severely punished."

He points in the opposite direction and shoos us with his hands, back the way we came. I pick up Edith and walk ahead of him, with the little ones.

"Come back tomorrow morning, with clean clothes," he says, and he turns to climb the steps of the headquarters building. We walk on toward home. Home? Three sleeping mats full of bedbugs? The only thing that has ever made it home is Mam, and she is not there. I have never felt so alone, and so afraid.

The next day, Mrs. K. offers to take Marijke and René to the nuns and to watch Edith. She is not one of those who was caught giggling and simpering over the tarot cards, so I accept her kindness.

As soon as breakfast is over, I fold a clean dress, with clean underpants inside, and I am off for the first delivery. I have never seen the solitary confinement cells close up. There is an opening at the bottom of the cell, where things can be passed in and out. I am able to see her through a slit window in the upper part of the cell. When she looks at me, her eyes are filled with sadness. They seem to plead for help from God. It is very hard for me to look at Mam without any emotion, but I have to stay strong or she will be punished. I put the clean clothes down and walk on by.

As the days and then the weeks go by, we may not be allowed to speak, but Mam's eyes are like magnets. We learn to communicate through our eyes. That's how she tells me one day she has something for me in the clothes I am picking up. I fly home, to find the treasure. I am so excited.

I go straight to the water spigot on the side of the house, where we wash clothes. Whatever Mam has hidden, I cannot wait to see it, to hold it and love it. I unfold the bundle—the dress has been folded over the underpants, as usual, but I find nothing else. I shake the dress, but nothing falls out. I turn everything inside out, but I find nothing. Tears come. Perhaps I misunderstood the message in her eyes. I am so disappointed.

I reach for the washboard that leans against the wall and then I turn on the water. I kneel down to put the dress under the stream of water and start the scrubbing. The fabric is so thin you can almost see through it. I must be very careful or I will push my hand right through the cloth. I wish I had some soap. I start at the neckline and work my way down. When I get to the hem, my hand wraps around a small lump. I jump to my feet. I have found it! Mam has sewn something into the hem of her dress. My mind leaps to the needle she always kept under her lapel. A tiny little needle—they did not find it when they arrested her.

I scratch at the thread that bastes the hem closed until I can raise it and bite through it. I sit back down to open the hem, and I find the little handkerchief that I made for her when I was six years old. She had it in her pocket when she was taken to the jail. I see a message embroidered on it. Somehow, Mam has taken green threads out of one of her dresses to stitch these words:

My darling children,
Have you been good?
Be loving to each other
watch over baby sister
Does little brother enjoy school?
Does Mieke go also?
Pray that Mam comes home soon
Till I see you again, Darlings.

A message from Mam! It is the most beautiful thing I have ever seen, but is a joy I can share with no one. I will keep the handkerchief in my pocket day and night, both to wring comfort from it and to protect Mam from being found out. I am prepared to swallow the evidence before I let her jailers know what she has done.

I hug the handkerchief to my chest, and I think my heart must be getting ready to fly into a million pieces, I have such happy pain.

Chapter 21.
Freedom at a Price

The summer of 1945: World War II was spinning toward a dramatic finish, but in Camp Halmaheira we still clung to the edges of survival, unaware that victory was at hand. I still scrounged for food, but I had to be more cautious than ever, for what would happen to the children if I were caught and imprisoned? I worried constantly about the little ones and about Mam. Through the small opening at the bottom of her cell door, I caught glimpses of her horribly swollen legs, and I knew she had beriberi. I had no idea of the other problems she was suffering.

Let her go, my mind would rage at the Kempeitai; we can't go on like this. But I became a master at not showing my feelings. I could not let Mam know how close I was to giving up. Then, on August 15th, two miracles happened, but I only knew about one of them. The other we would learn a few days later.

I am standing outside our house when I see trucks turning onto our street. More ragged, half-starved women and children coming in from other camps. The trucks roll by, but one stops a few houses away and begins to unload. A woman jumps down from the tailgate, and a guard points in the direction of our house and gives her a shove. She does not have any children with her, and she looks stronger than most of the others. Perhaps Mam would have been stronger if she had not given most of her food to us. The woman walks toward me. But wait, she walks like—

"Tante Zus!" I scream at the very same moment the woman screams, "Ilse!"

We are in each other's arms in a second, crying and hugging each other. Thank you, thank you, thank you, I am thinking. Then I realize that my aunt, while she is hugging me, is calling, "Mies! Mies!"

I back away, wiping my teary face with my hands. Tante Zus is looking around, thinking her older sister must be nearby. I tell her the terrible truth of what has become of Mam. For the rest of the day she watches after the little ones and I sleep. It is the first rest I have had for weeks. Even the itching cannot disturb me.

Early the next day Tante Zus goes to the Kempeitai headquarters to ask permission to accompany me to Mam's cell. Oh, she is so brave.

We walk together arm in arm, and when we get to the cell, we dare to take an extra moment at the slit window. When Mam sees her sister, her eyes grow huge and tears start rolling down her face–the first time I have seen Mam cry since she was put into solitary confinement. Then she collapses into a heap on the floor of the little oven. Tante Zus and I run to find a guard.

"Oh please, gunjin-san—my mother has fainted in her cell. Please go see what has happened," I beg.

The soldier shoves me aside, but he goes to my mother's cell, and then he disappears into a back door of the headquarters building. Zus and I stand near the cell, but we are afraid to say anything to Mam in case it will cause her grief later. Finally the soldier comes back and unlocks the cell. We can take her home, he says.

Mam is unconscious, unable to stand. We have to lift her up and carry her out of that hell box. She is rail thin, but her legs are so swollen from the beriberi she is almost too heavy for the two of us to carry. Carefully, we inch our way down the hill with her between us, our arms under her shoulders and under her knees. Her head lolls backward, but we can't help it; we get her home as best we can. We lay her on her sleeping mat.

My aunt prepares to wash Mam and put her into clean clothes. She removes my mother's dress. "Oh, dear God, what have they done to her?" she gasps. We see the results of the many beatings. Because of neglect and malnutrition, the wounds have not healed. She has been in terrible pain, but her eyes have protected me from knowing what I could not have borne. My darling, loving, courageous, precious mother. She has suffered so.

Two days, in and out of consciousness. Mam knows we are here, but she is too weak to do anything but open her eyes only slightly. Sometimes her mouth curves into the hint of a smile. Sometimes a nod, barely a movement. She tries to stay awake, but the eyes close again.

But she is here! My mother is here, and I do not leave her side except to go to the squatting holes. Tante Zus takes care of the children and brings me food. I try to put food and water into Mam's mouth, but not much goes down except for a little of the liquid, and often she chokes on that.

Then the bleeding begins, and we must put pads under her. Everything we have left in the pillowcases, including the pillowcases themselves are put to use to soak up the blood. Tante Zus runs to wash out one pad as another is turning red. We cannot stop the hemorrhaging. Bleeding hemorrhoids, Tante Zus says. Is this just one more way to die at Camp Halmaheira? Oh, please no, please, please, please.

The blood loss keeps her unconscious most of the time, and I am grateful she is not in pain. I know I am going to lose her, and I weep until my ribs ache. If only I could talk to her one last time. "Oh Mam, I love you so much," I say over and over, when I have enough breath to speak.

Finally, I receive one last gift from my mother. It is early in the morning, around two o'clock, I think. Mam is lying across our mattresses, her head in my lap. The children are asleep and Zus naps beside me. Because the end is near, we have left the ceiling light on all night, and I look at Mam in the soft light. I study her face with my eyes, and then I run my fingers, oh so lightly, over her forehead, her cheeks, her nose, her lips, her chin. I memorize every line, every pore. She opens her eyes wide and smiles at me.

"Ilse, honey, you are so grown up, and you are so pretty. Give baby Edith lots of love, and when she is big enough to understand, tell her about me—will you?"

My throat closes up, I cannot speak. If I try, my voice will come out in a wail, and I must not upset my mother with my own pain. But I cannot keep the tears from streaming. I bend to kiss her and our eyes meet. I understand what her eyes are saying, that she is not afraid to die, but she is sorry to leave us, her children. A tear rolls down her cheek. She asks for Zus, who leans in close, to hear the whispered words.

"Take care of my children, Zus."

"Of course, Mies—"

"Promise, Zus, promise!" Mam's eyes flare. It is like she has Tante Zus in a strong grip and will not let go until she is satisfied with the answer.

Tante Zus clenches her teeth and breathes hard. I know she is fighting the sobs that are pushing against her throat.

"I promise, Mies. I will never leave the children. I promise."

Mam's eyes close and her breathing gets louder and slower. The children are awake, and I answer their questions, but all I am really hearing is Mam's breathing in, breathing out.

At three o'clock in the morning, Mam's breath stops. I kiss her for the very last time, and then I think I am going to open my mouth and howl like an animal. I feel it pushing up from my stomach. Then, in an instant, I am filled with an overwhelming sense of peace. She is no longer suffering. Thank you, thank you, thank you. It is August 17, 1945.

Now it is our turn to follow the grobak to the gate. Tante Zus gets one of the woven bamboo mats and rolls it carefully around Mam's tortured body. We shuffle along behind the grobak. Tante Zus holds René's hand, and I carry Edith. Marijke walks between us. Into the Kempeitai compound, past the headquarters building where I pleaded for my mother's return, past the solitary confinement cells which took her life, up to the gate she passed through so many times to go to work. Again she passes through, but this time she will not have to come back. She is on the free side of the fence for good.

Maria Christina Elizabeth Fiedeldij (later Evelijn Veere) at eighteen years old. Born in 1904 in Midjokderto, Java, Dutch East Indies.

Mies and Henk Evelijn Veere with family in Medan, Sumatra before WWII. Mies is seated. Standing, left to right: Henk, his sister Annie Gerrits, Ruud Doyer, and Zus Fiedeldij Doyer, Maria's younger sister.

*In Medan, Sumatra, 1941, the children of Maria and Hendrik
Evelijn Veere: (from the left) René (age 2), Ilse (age 8), and Marijke
(age 4).*

The handkerchief with an embroidered message, Maria's legacy of love and courage, left to her children at Camp Halmaheira in 1945.

Hendrik Evelijn Veere and his second wife, Noes—the lady in the pavilion—at their remarriage in Amsterdam in 1951.

The wedding of Ilse Evelijn Veere and Jan Smit in Amsterdam in 1954.

The Evelijn Veere children, as they gather for a family celebration in Washington State: in front, René (on left) and "baby" Edith; in back, Ilse (on left) and Marijke.

Marijke represents the Evelijn Veere children as she places flowers upon their mother's final resting place in Semarang, Java.

Chapter 22.
Rumors

One morning very soon after my mother's death, roll call was abandoned. We milled about, ready to line up, but no one showed up to count us and yell threats at us. The rumor began to dart about the camp, *"Perang sudah habis."* The war is over.

❦

I hear the rumor but I do not believe. Nothing can break through my grief, certainly not an empty rumor that has no evidence to back it up. When we go for our breakfast a kitchen server covers our bubur dedek with sweet coconut milk. Oh, it is so delicious.

But still I do not believe. All I can think of is the way Mam's eyes would be smiling, to see us slurping up the sweet stuff. It is hard to see the smiling eyes past the death-haunted eyes of her last days.

Even when I see the guards just standing around, not yelling or kicking, I do not believe. Wrapped in my grief, I care about neither abuse nor the lack of it. Our dinner that evening tastes better than usual—salt, maybe—and the portions are much larger.

The next day we hear the hum of airplanes, and we look up to see one coming in low. British, some of the women say, and no one runs for shelter, so neither do I. I watch pamphlets flutter downward in the warm air currents, and when they settle to the ground, we pick them up. In three languages—English, Dutch and Bahasa Maleis—they tell us the war is over, and then I believe. But I am in for a shock.

"...August 15, 1945," the pamphlet says. Emperor Hirohito announced the surrender of Japanese forces on August 15th? Mam was still alive. The war was ending as we carried her out of that cell.

Surrounded by hundreds of prisoners shouting and hugging—some of them hugging me—I am alone and sobbing. Oh, Mam, I am thinking. If only you had known. If only I could have told you. If only I could have followed you through that gate, to see where they put you.

Tante Zus appears at my side. She holds me close, and I know she is thinking the same thoughts. All over again, my grief is squeezing my heart until I'm sure it will burst.

"Tante," we hear Marijke say. "Another airplane!"

We look up to see a plane, marked like the first one. When it is overhead, we see something dropping from its belly, and parachutes are popping open, poof, poof, poof. As they drift closer, we see huge rope nets full of something that looks like cans.

"Food!" someone shouts, and we all run for cover to keep from getting squashed by falling food.

Oh, yes, I can believe the war is over when food cans instead of bombs are dropping out of an airplane. The rope nets hit the ground and open up. The cans are free for the taking. We all run out from under our shelters.

I gather as many cans as I am able to put into the hammock I have made of my skirt. I don't care that my underpants are in plain sight. Much more has been in plain sight time and again in this place. I run my precious load into our room and dump it onto my mattress. Marijke runs in too, with as many cans as she can hold, and René is right behind her, holding out a can for my approval.

"Read it," he demands.

I must study the words. Reading has become difficult for me. "*Pinda kaas*," I tell René. Peanut butter. René's eyes light up and Marijke claps her hands. They are old enough to remember peanut butter. Then I read the contents of the other cans. *Wafels*, those wonderful sandwich cookies with honey pressed between the layers; *lever pastij*, liver spread; *kleine worstje,* little sausages. We are standing in the middle of a feast, but it is all trapped inside thick cans, and we did not see any can openers roll out of the rope basket.

Tante Zus comes to the rescue. She adds her armload of cans to the pile and then she reaches into her pocket and produces a knife and a rock. In less than a minute, we are eating little sausages. Tante Zus is very resourceful.

"We cannot eat it all at once, or we will be sick," our aunt warns. We all agree, although I am thinking I would like to try a little of everything. We sort through the cans and decide on one more to eat now. We will save the rest for later.

When we finish the feast, I realize that my mother's pale grey face and haunted eyes have not been hovering in my mind's eye since the parachutes delivered their astonishing cargo. Nor have I thought of the blood-soaked pads that we removed from beneath her so many times as she bled to death in her last hours.

"Oh, Mam," I cry, guilty that she has not been a part of this, even in my mind. I weep until I fall asleep on my mat, in the middle of the morning, surrounded by cans with words that I can barely read stenciled on their sides.

A few days go by—long enough for the canned provisions to be almost used up. The prisoners—or are we now just residents?—are called together in the commons where punishments are carried out and important announcements are made. Tante Zus stands behind us, her arms making a protective circle around us. I thank God constantly for my aunt. I am sure Mam's angel must have sent her.

We wait for a long time, wondering what is going to happen. The Japanese guards mill around, waiting along with us. Then the camp commander, Hasegawa, marches up, parting the crowd. A Javanese man accompanies him. The native jumps up onto a concrete block and begins to shout so all of us can hear.

"You are allowed to move about freely. Today the gates will be open," he says in Bahasa Maleis.

My ears hear, but do not absorb. The gates will be open? When just a few days ago, I was not permitted to follow the grobak to see where my mother was buried?

"You may go into the city or into the countryside, but you must return to the camp before dusk."

Return to the camp? Why would we ever want to return to this place?

"It is not safe for you outside these gates."

And it has been safe for us inside these gates? I almost laugh, but I know better than to call attention to myself. The war may be over, but the guards still wear swords and steel boots. Then the Javanese speaker tells us what is happening outside Camp Halmaheira.

On August 17th, the very day my mother died, someone named Sukarno declared the independence of the Republic of Indonesia, and now a new war is going on throughout our country. He tells us that *pemudas*—young "freedom fighters" are roaming about. They shout *"merdeka!"* which means "freedom," and they are armed with machetes and with spears poisoned with *bambu runtjing*. We are their target, the Dutch and the part-Dutch.

By the time this Javanese finishes talking it is clear we have two choices: trust the Japanese here to protect us, or trust the Javanese out there to show us mercy. It is a decision I am not prepared to make, and again I thank God for my aunt.

The next morning I see Tante Zus packing a few things into a gunnysack. I pay little attention to what goes into the sack. She calls us together after breakfast—a good breakfast with coconut and nutmeg on top of the porridge.

"Come," my aunt says. "We shall see what the world is like outside this fence."

I doubt whether we will be going far since machetes and bambu runtjing are waiting for us out there. I still do not know what to think of the present state of affairs.

"Ilse, you carry Edith," she says. "I will carry the bag and watch out for the other two."

Off we go, to the gate. I am thinking of the last time I stood before the gate, and I wish Mam could be with us, alive and well. Oh, how desperately I wish it.

As we approach the gate, a soldier calls to us.

"It is dangerous out there, *ojyousan*," he says. I cannot believe my ears, to hear a Japanese speaking politely to my aunt, calling her "miss."

"Yes, I know," she answers.

"Take this with you." He hands her a billy club. "You can use it to protect yourself and the children from dogs. Or other wild animals." I know what he really means—those freedom fighters who want to whack off our heads.

"Thank you," says Tante Zus. "It will be useful."

"Do not go near a *désa*," he says. He is talking about the primitive native villages that are built up around the countryside. "They are full of pemudas that would want you dead."

I can't help but shudder at the thought of anyone wanting me dead.

As we turn to walk through the open gate, the soldier calls, "Be sure to come back before dusk!"

My aunt does not turn around. She leads us through the wide opening. We are free, at last. Tante Zus throws the gunnysack over her shoulder and strikes out, fast. We have to scramble to keep up with her. It is as if she is afraid the Japanese will break their promise and come after us, like the Pharaoh when Moses led his people out of Egypt. But we have no Red Sea, only the Semarang River which used to receive the waste from the toilets of Halmaheira before they were plugged with concrete.

At a safe distance, with no one following us but other prisoners, Tante Zus stops and turns around. We can still see the sign stretched across the top of the wide gate: Camp Halmaheira.

"We will never go back," she says.

And we didn't. Instead we struck out on an incredible journey that was filled with every bit as much terror and fear as we had experienced at the hands of the Japanese. And what about the Japanese, these Kempeitai who tortured us, starved us, and killed my mother? They finally made good in their role as protectors—this time, of the Europeans and Eurasians in their care. Why? The answer might lie in the rigid training of the Japanese military. They were trained to obey authority. Our side—the Allies, the Dutch, were now in authority.

Chapter 23.
The Goat

To appreciate the story of our trek, you must understand the geography of Java. First, the north central coast is a plateau, a dry plain by comparison with the mountainous regions further south. Second, the dry season usually peaks in August, and 1945 was no exception. So when we crossed the Semarang River along with hundreds of other camp refugees, we headed east into a blistering hot plateau in the throes of a drought. I am not sure if Tante Zus had a destination in mind at first. I think the only direction she knew to go at that moment was "away"—away from Camp Halmaheira and Semarang, the city that hosted it.

Most of the crowd has turned off on one road or another. I think some have turned back, but we keep walking, and a few Hollanders walk with us. The road ends, but we just walk on through grassland. The countryside is oh, so quiet. And oh, so hot. The grass is getting hard to walk on—taller and thicker, and we are barefooted. Our shoes wore out a long time ago. Then out of nowhere, a path appears before us. It leads us through thick alang alang—a good thing, as the razor edges of alang alang would cut our feet.

The path ends at several rows of ditches we must cross if we are to continue in an easterly direction. Tante Zus stops and looks in all directions. Behind us is Halmaheira. To the left is the sea. To the right, she says, are other cities. Straight ahead is open country.

"Let's move on," she says.

The Hollanders agree, and we tramp down into the first of the dry ditches. When we cross the last one, we are in an open field. The grass is short, but tough and pointed, and it hurts my feet. As usual I am carrying Edith. She is a tiny two-year-old, but still heavy for me, so I shift her around and she rides piggyback. René is brave, but Marijke starts to whine.

"Hush, Marijke," I tell her. "Your feet will toughen up. Be glad you do not have to carry Edith." When our feet begin to bleed I feel sorry for Marijke, but I do not want the whining to start again, so I say nothing.

Tante Zus finally stops in the middle of the field. Everyone is glad for the rest.

She opens the gunnysack and takes out cans of water. Oh, so good. I lie flat down in the grass. I could easily sleep.

"We are too much out in the open here," Tante Zus says. "We need to move on." We do, and I am very grateful to one of the Dutch ladies who picks up Edith.

As we walk I remember Kaliagnet, long ago, on the island of Madura, when we walked to the beach together, Mam and Pap, Marijke and I, before René was born. The beach was so white it almost hurt our eyes. They mined salt there, where the ocean brought it to the shore. Pap wanted me to be a good swimmer, but I was still a little nervous about putting my head under water. He would swim out to the deep water with me on his back. He was very strong. Always he would promise not to dive under the water, and always I would believe him. But then he would say, "Here we go, Ilse," and he would hold my feet while he dove down, taking me under the water with him. When we came up, he would be laughing and I would be coughing and sputtering and crying. I wonder why I always believed him. I wonder why he thought it was funny. But I did finally learn to hold my breath and let it out slowly through my mouth, and now I am a very good swimmer. I suppose Pap had something to do with that. I wish I could jump in some water right now. Oh, but I am so hot.

I think of other times, to keep my mind off the heat and my bleeding feet. Like the times Pap would lie down on his stomach and invite me to draw pictures on his back, for him to guess. I would put great effort into my pictures—the school building, complete with playground. Or Mam's favorite teapot, with little blue Chinese figures and trees. But he never guessed it right because he always went to sleep before the picture was done. Mam never went to sleep during our picture-guessing games. I am glad I can think of Mam during the happy times. I wish I could lie down right now and let Marijke or René draw pictures on my back. I would never guess them, though, because I would be asleep in an instant.

We keep walking the rest of the day, our first day of freedom. When we rest, Tante Zus gives us water, but not much food from the cans she has packed in the gunnysack. Too much to eat would make us sick in this fierce heat. Besides, we have only a few cans left.

When the sun disappears over the horizon, we find a clump of trees and bushes to shelter us while we sleep. Half of our water is used up. Tante Zus says she did not reckon with the dryness of the land so now we must ration the water. I explain what that means to Marijke and René. Edith is too little to understand.

We are very hungry. I am thinking of the cans of peanut butter and of sausages I saw in the bag, but Tante Zus brings out cold rice—she raided the central kitchen before we left the camp. It tastes good, and all the better for being eaten outside, in freedom. We sleep under the open sky, hearing night sounds of nature that I cannot identify, but they sound soft and friendly to me. With no streetlights or city lights to interfere with the darkness, the stars are brilliant. If only Mam could be with us, I think for the thousandth time. If only I knew where she was buried. I go to sleep making pictures in the sky by drawing lines from star to star. Pap and I used to do that while he taught me about astronomy.

I wake very early to the sound of roosters crowing not far away. In the morning light we can see the désa that we missed in the darkness the night before. Fortunately the native village missed us, too.

"Okay, everyone, we must stay low and be totally silent," Tante Zus whispers to all of us circled around her. "We must not let anyone in the village see us or hear us. Do you understand?"

Everyone nods. I understand, all right. I understand there are people in that désa who want to kill us. I am angry that we are still victims. We are supposed to be free. Ha!

We make a wide circle around the little thatched huts clustered in the shadow of the hill we slept on. The grass is tall, and the adults hunch over to hide their silhouettes. We move slowly to keep from making the grass wave when there is no wind. It is difficult, but we manage to pass by the désa, and we put it far behind us. We tramp on through most of the day, putting distance between us and Camp Halmaheira and between us and the désa that we narrowly escaped.

We are walking alongside a *rimber*, an unkempt patch of land which looks like it might once have been a cornfield. Probably someone once planted corn there for their livestock, but I see no hut nearby and certainly no désa, thank heaven. We are tired and very, very hungry. Tante Zus suddenly stops. "Sh!" she says, and puts up her hand to silence everyone. Then I hear it. A bell. Tante Zus signals us to stay behind, and she creeps alongside the rimber to the top of a little rise, her billy club in hand. She is ready to do battle with a freedom fighter. But instead of attacking a pemuda, she turns around and walks back, smiling.

"A goat," she whispers. "Come and look, but be quiet."

We all go to the top of the hill, and sure enough, there is a nanny goat standing in the ditch, munching on the dead leaves of an old cornstalk. Dangling from her neck is a bell which is fastened to a rope that is loose at the other end.

"That is our next meal," Tante Zus whispers. She does not want to alarm the goat, I think. "Ilse, I am going over to that goat, and when I call you, you must come running as fast as you can."

I nod. My aunt slowly, slowly, walks up to the goat, making soothing sounds— goat-friendly sounds, I would say. The creature just keeps munching until Tante Zus comes up beside her, and then the goat tilts her head to the side a bit and looks up, like she is asking, "Who are you?"

Tante Zus whips the billy club out and hits that goat in the side of the head with a mighty thwap. "Ilse!" she calls as the goat falls to the ground. I am there in a blink of the poor goat's eye, just as Tante Zus pulls a knife out of her pocket and slits its neck. Blood spurts.

"Ilse, I am going to open her up, and when the stomach pops out, you must reach in and grab the little round bag behind it."

"Why?" I ask, still in shock over the goat's bloody death.

"It is the gall bladder. It's full of bile. Pull it out, or the meat will be spoiled. Do you understand?"

I nod, but what I see next almost makes me forget what I am supposed to do. Tante Zus slits the goat from neck to belly, fast, with one strong swipe of her knife. More blood. I am dumfounded. Sure enough, the stomach pops out and I see a round bag in the bloody mess behind it. Tante Zus pulls the two sides of the opening apart, grunting with the effort.

"Grab it, Ilse! Don't let it break! Pull it out of there!"

I do, and I wonder where Tante Zus learned to do such things. And where did she get the strength? I sit back in the blood soaked ditch and wonder how I managed to reach in the warm insides of a just-killed goat and do what I just did.

The slaughter is just the first of a lot of bloody work that needs to be done. The rest of the guts must be pulled out. The head comes off, and then Tante Zus starts pulling the skin away from the neck. Little by little, knife stroke by knife stroke, Tante Zus cuts the skin right off that animal until she gets down past its haunches. Finally the skinny part of the legs come off, and Nanny is ready for roasting.

One of the Hollanders starts a fire down in a gully where it won't be easily seen. The women pile some rocks just so, to support what is left of the poor creature up over the fire and we watch the flesh cook. They flop it over a few times, to let it cook on all sides, and finally we eat fresh meat for the first time in over two years. It is the most delicious meal I have ever eaten. We decide to end our walking for the day, and we lie down with our full bellies, to rest in the shade of the thirsty trees in the dry gully.

"My gut hurts!" René announces. He rises, bends over, and heaves up the goat which just went down a short time ago. I gag, but I make it to the outside of the tree circle before I lose my meal. The others, too—it is an epidemic of throwing up.

Tante Zus is laughing as she retches. "I guess it's too rich for us," she says when she can get her breath enough to talk.

Sick or not, we get up the next morning and eat some more, but not quite so much this time. Sadly, with no way to refrigerate it, we have to leave the rest of the goat. But Nanny has given us a great boost and stamina to move on. The question is, where are we going?

Chapter 24.
Désa Angel

Tante Zus had a destination: Oro-oro Ombo in the mountains of the Soember Brantas where Tante Annie and Oom Theo lived. If Oom Theo had not been conscripted, if Tante Annie and the children had not been forced into internment, and if the pemudas had not driven them out or worse yet, slaughtered them, then they would help us. A lot of "ifs," but Tante Zus focused on the positive. "We will sleep in real beds," she said, "with clean sheets!"

Tante Annie was my father's sister, and her husband, Theo Gerrits, ran a coffee plantation. The Soember Brantas was a pleasant place to escape the pounding heat of the dry season, and I remembered visiting there many times. My adult memory recalls gladiolas, however, not coffee. Fields of gladiolas in bloom took my breath away, the beauty of wide stripes of purple, yellow, white, red, pink, and orange that led all the way to a little girl's horizon.

But neither coffee nor flowers were on my mind as we trudged along. We were not sure exactly how far we were from Oro-oro Ombo, nor did we know exactly how to get there. Of course it would have been simple to drop into a town and ask someone, "What is the best way to get to Oro-oro Ombo?" Then, set on the right road, we could have walked there quite easily, or perhaps gotten rides with farmers going in the same direction. But we did not dare to drop into a town, nor did we dare to use the roads.

So on through the countryside we walked in the hot sun, over tough native grasses, up and down hillocks, through and around thickets of scrub brush, in the east-southeasterly direction of the Soember Brantas. The Hollanders stuck with us, I guess, for lack of any plan of their own. They were very nice, and I was glad for the help with Edith.

In honesty, the trek has become a blur of memories. How many days? I forget. How many Hollanders? I forget. How far? I never really knew. But the specific memories that survived the experience remain vivid.

We are two, maybe three days from the nanny goat. I am trying to remember what it is like to slide into a bed between smooth, cool sheets. I am actually trying to think of anything besides water. Even food does not occupy my thoughts the way a long drink of water does—glug, glug, glug, just tip up the cup and keep gulping until the water is gone.

We are lucky. We have seen no one who might want to harm us. We have seen no one, period. This is wilderness country. Even the bloodthirsty pemudas do not get this far away from civilization—and water. But there is always the danger that over the next little rise there might be a désa, or a band of pemudas out looking for Dutch blood.

We come to a stream bed, dry of course. Eucalyptus trees line the dry stream, waiting for the rainy season. Tante Zus stops and gathers us to her. It is so good to have a rest in the shade. The Hollanders gather in a group, too. I wonder what they have in the way of food and water. We have been sharing up until now, but I don't think anyone has anything left to share.

This is just a water stop. The sun is high overhead. Tante Zus brings out her last can of water, punches two little holes in the top, and gives the children and me a tiny sip. René and Edith whine. "More! More!" For the millionth time, she explains that we must not drink all of our water at once. She is too patient. I cannot stand any more of it, but I cannot shout, in case someone is close enough to hear. So my voice comes out in a hiss.

"Shut up! You know the answer already. Don't ask again or I shall slap you!"

"Ilse, you must be kind to the little ones," Tante Zus says.

"They are not so little," I tell her and then I glare at my sister Marijke who, for once, has not been complaining. She glares right back at me. I glance at René and Edith and I feel guilty. But I still glare at Marijke who tosses her head and looks away, with her nose up in the air.

I lie back on the dry grass and close my eyes. I don't want to go to sleep because I want to eavesdrop on what Tante Zus is saying to the Hollanders who are huddled in a circle.

"I have something to tell you," Tante Zus says. "I am very sorry about this, but it is a matter of survival, you know."

This sounds very serious. I open my eyes to peek at the grownups.

"We just can't go on together," Tante Zus tells them. "We are down to our last can of water, and I am going to have to ask for help in one of the désas."

Tante Zus doesn't have to explain that it is dangerous for us to travel with them. We might be able to pass for natives if

we keep our mouths shut—I am the only one who can speak
Maleis like a native. But the Hollanders' blue eyes and blond
hair, bleached even more blond by the sun, are like magnets to
the eye.

I can see that Tante Zus is trying to be strong. She is biting the insides of her cheeks, and I can see her chest rising and
falling with deep breathing, the kind that you do when you are
trying not to break out in sobs.

"If it weren't for the children—" she says. "I just can't risk
their getting caught, you know—" Then the tears come. Poor
Tante Zus. The women have been helpful to her. It will be hard
to go on alone.

They gather up their belongings. I hope they have water
in those bags. "God be with you," everyone says, and the
Hollanders turn back along the route we just took. I wonder
what their fate will be. For that matter, I wonder what our fate
will be. What if we don't find Tante Annie and Oom Theo? I
am crying, too.

When we have recovered enough to talk, Tante Zus gathers
us all around her.

"Children, you must listen carefully and promise me you
will do exactly as I say, if we run into anyone along the way."
She has our attention, even Edith's.

"We must act like we are Javanese on our way from one
désa to another. Just think like a native and act like one. Do
you understand?"

I understand. I have always been very good at play-acting.
Probably Marijke understands, but I am sure René and Edith
don't get it. Their society has been made up of armed guards
and prisoners. They would not know a native from a school
headmaster.

"Do you understand?" Tante Zus repeats, and we all nod our heads.

The afternoon drifts along. We plow through dry grass, mostly alang alang which parts before us and closes up behind us. The sharp edges hardly bother us any more. Our feet have toughened up and we have learned how to pick them up and put them down just so, to avoid being sliced.

The sun is getting lower. It will sink before long, and we will have some relief from the heat, but still no water. We walk and we walk, mountains far off to the right, sun now at our backs. The children, including Marijke, are whimpering, and I have no strength left to be disgusted with them. I want to whimper, too. I am beginning to wonder if we have any hope at all of doing anything but walking the rest of our lives. Or if we will ever eat again. Or if we will just dry up like dead leaves and blow away.

Tante Zus has given up saying encouraging little things to us, like "soon we will find a river," or "just a little longer, my sweets, and we will stop to rest and listen to the cicadas sing." Finally she does say, as we struggle across the rough terrain, "See the trees at the top of that little hill? That will be a good place to stop for the night. Just a little further, schatjes, and you can rest."

"I'm hungry," whines René, and Edith chimes in with, "Me, too." Marijke and I just look at each other. I am sure we are thinking the same thing—they are such babies. It makes it worse when you talk about it.

"Well, perhaps a chicken will cross our path," says Tante Zus, and I actually produce a little saliva at the thought of roasted chicken meat. Spit doesn't come easy when you are drying up from thirst. It feels good.

Tante Zus is first to reach the trees. She has Edith on her back. Suddenly they disappear as she drops to the ground.

"Tante Zus, Tante Zus," I call, and I break into as much of a run as I can manage. She sits up and waves her arms, crossing her hands in front of her face in a "No, no—stop!" gesture. With Edith hanging over her arm like a handbag, she scrambles back down the hill, to warn us.

"Hush," she whispers. "There is a désa at the bottom of the hill, on the other side. We can go to the trees, but we must be very quiet."

We creep the rest of the way and sure enough, we see the little village right there in front of us. We lie low in the grass. We see people moving around in the village. Some of the men carry long spears. I am sure we are looking at freedom fighters who would make short work of us if they knew we were here.

One little hut is on the edge of the désa, all by itself. In the fading light we can see a woman sitting on a low stool in front of her door. We are near enough to see she is very old, with wispy white hair and a scrawny neck. We watch her for several minutes. No one else goes in or comes out of her tiny hut. Apparently she lives alone.

"I am going to go down to talk with her," Tante Zus whispers. "Maybe she will give us food and water."

I am afraid. What will happen to us if Tante Zus is caught by the evil ones in the village? She reassures me. "We have come this far, Ilse. I do not believe God means to forsake us now. But I will wait until it is darker."

Soon the hillside is dark enough for Tante Zus to blend into the landscape. The younger ones are already asleep. They are so tired at the end of a walking day, they can sleep the minute their heads come to rest on anything—a rock, a clump of dirt, a heap of dry grass. Tante Zus taps my shoulder and pulls me away from the sleeping children to give me instructions.

"Now, Ilse, you and the children must stay very still," she whispers. "No one will know you are here. If I do not return, you must leave before the sun rises in the morning. No matter what you might see or hear, you must stay right here and leave before dawn."

"But Tante Zus, where will we go?" I am next to tears, and my whispered words sound like dots and dashes. My chest is clamped up with fear.

"Silly girl, you will go on in the direction we have been going—toward the sun in the morning, mountains on your right. I am sure Oro-oro Ombo is in those near mountains." I don't ask the other questions that are on my mind. What will we eat? What will we do about water? We have eaten bugs before, and we can certainly do it again. But water is hard to find when it's not there.

"I am sure you will find a river when you get into the mountains," she says. Tante Zus has read my mind. I wonder, though, if it is that simple, then why do we need to ask the old woman for help? But I do not ask.

My aunt starts down the hill, and by the time she gets to the hut it is too dark to see much except the faint outline of two figures—hers and the old woman's. At least no one is screaming or calling for the pemudas to come and lop off my aunt's head. That is a good sign. I wait. I can see nothing now in the darkness between us and the hut on the edge of the désa, but my eyes stay wide open looking for Tante Zus to reappear. Please, please, please, I pray.

My prayers are answered. I do not see my aunt until she is an arm's length away.

"The old grandmother will help us," she says. "We can stay in her hut tonight, but we must be gone before morning light. She could be killed for helping us."

Thank you, thank you, thank you, I whisper, as much to the old lady as to God. We wake the children and get them on their feet. As usual, I pick up Edith.

"Careful, don't trip," Tante Zus says as she leads us toward the désa.

The old woman is already busy at the anglo when we enter. I watch her face, in the light of the kerosene lamp. Every millimeter in bird-foot wrinkles, only two or three snaggly, brown teeth, eyes clouded over with thick cataracts. But she is beautiful to me, as she prepares our food. It is just like the food my babu kokki cooked. Fried *tempeh*—soybean cakes; steamed *kangkung*—spinach-like greens, seasoned with tangy spices; and my favorite, *pisang goreng*—fried bananas. She could have sold these delicacies at the Pasar Baru! We drink water which comes from a rain barrel at the side of the hut. I wonder where it comes from, in this dry terrain, but I gulp it gratefully.

At last, we bed down on the dirt floor of the hut. Not the same as clean sheets, but adequate, and offered by a kind human being who cares whether we live or die.

Chapter 25.
Pemuda Terror

The Bersiap Period of Indonesian history lasted from August to December of 1945. Short, but fierce. Every real or perceived colonial injustice was to be avenged, in the minds of the young native islanders crying "merdeka" and "*bersiap!*" which means "be prepared!" Be prepared for what? Home rule or a bloodbath?

In fairness, the leaders who declared independence on the day my mother died probably did not mean for the bloodbath to happen, but they could not control it. Two revolutions were taking place—the military one between the Netherlands and the new Republic of Indonesia, and the social one between native islanders and their former rulers. Never mind that most of the former rulers they attacked were defenseless Dutch and Indies, mostly women and children who had no place to go for protection.

Our old benefactor sent us off from her désa hut with a bag full of food, wrapped the old way in banana leaves, jars full of water, and a clear explanation of the situation we were in.

"You must not get caught by the pemudas," she says in the Pasar Maleis spoken by our babu kokki. She keeps her voice low. "If you were lucky, they would kill you instantly, probably with their machetes. More likely, they would torture you first and have their way with all of you, even the little boy."

"But we are not Hollanders," my aunt says, frowning.

"They will not be impressed by your dark skin, Miss. They hate you mixed bloods even more than they hate the Hollanders."

"But why, Grandmother?" I blurt out in Pasar Maleis. "How could the sons and grandsons of my babu kokki hate me?"

Oh, oh, the secret is out. I can feel Tante Zus's eyes burrowing into my back. Old Grandmother breaks into a toothless smile.

"Ah, so you speak Pasar," she says, "like me."

"Well, a little," I admit, wondering why I feel so uncomfortable. Pap is the one who made the law against speaking Pasar Maleis, and he's not around.

"Since you asked so prettily, I will try to explain," she says. Her face is serious again. "These young hot bloods are angry because you turned against us and married with the Dutch to help them make slaves out of your own people—"

"Me? But I didn't—" I am sputtering with the unfairness. "My babu kokki—" Tante Zus cuts me off with a shake of her head. I guess this is not the right time to explain how I feel about the kokki. But I am indignant. Babu Kokki may have been a servant, but she was certainly not a slave, and I loved her as much as I loved my grandmothers who, incidentally, married Dutch men, but they didn't make slaves out of anyone. I think it, but I don't say it.

"I understand," says my aunt to the old grandmother.

"One more thing," says the old woman. "The pemudas have small camps in the forests where you are going. It is where they hide from the English and the Dutch soldiers. Take care to avoid them."

"We will be very careful," promises my aunt.

Tante Zus bows to the old grandmother, showing her respect. Marijke and I bow too, in the traditional way, palms together, fingers up, elbows out. It is so different from the bowing that was forced upon us by the Japanese in Camp Halmaheira. I want to hug the old lady, even though she thinks I made her a slave, but I am afraid it would be too forward. So I just bow again, to show my gratitude. *"Treemakasi banjak,"* I say. Thank you. I am already thinking about the pisang goreng wrapped up in the gunnysack.

"Go with Allah," she says. "And do not make a sound."

Marijke gives Edith a boost so I can carry her, piggyback, and Tante Zus takes René on her back. She picks up the treasure bag of food and without a sound, we slip out of the hut and up over the hill. It is still the dark of the night and the footing is hard, but the stars give a little light for us to escape by. A sliver of moon is on its way down over the horizon. Oh, are we not lucky to have found someone to help us? We are rich with food and water now, and surely we will find Tante Annie's house before too long.

I wish I could have used the rain barrel water to get clean. Even in Camp Halmaheira, I was never as filthy as I am now. I smell of sweat and bathrooming, and the lice have multiplied so much I can pull a dozen nits off one strand of hair. Marijke and I have not played our hair game since we left the camp. We have no sisir-sirit to nudge the lice out of their comfortable homes. But I can put the lice out of my mind and replace them with thoughts of pisang goreng for lunch. Or perhaps a snack later in the morning.

Tante Zus leads us back over the ridge and down the hill again, to a dirt road. I am surprised. Isn't this dangerous? But I am too happy thinking of the feast in the gunnysack to worry about the pemudas and their hatred. And I am glad that Tante Zus can take Edith, now that René can walk on his own. He is only six, but he is a good walker.

Walking on a road instead of having to select every step, we put distance between us and the old lady's hut, toward the sunrise when it comes.

"I did not know you could speak in the Pasar dialect, Ilse," my aunt says when it is safe to talk.

I feel a blush work its way up my neck, and my face is hot. I should have stayed silent back there at the old grand-mother's house.

"You sound like a native Javanese," she says.

I feel some pride that I speak Pasar Maleis so well, but I'm not sure if I should say thank you.

"That could come in handy, you know," she says.

No, I didn't know. "How is that, Tante?"

"You could help us pass as natives if we should need to do so."

My stomach tightens at the idea of having to even see a native, let alone say anything, after the warning the old grand-mother gave us. "Hmph," I grunt, and we walk on in silence. Pisang goreng leads me on. I realize we are walking uphill, and the forest is getting thicker on either side the road. Pink light from the rising sun creeps up behind mountains which are now ahead of us. The brighter orange light that comes before the sun itself is now a bit to our left. I am puzzled.

"Let's rest a minute." Tante Zus leads us off the road to a cluster of bushes that will hide us.

"Tante Zus, have we gone in the wrong direction? And why are we using the road? Aren't we afraid of the pemudas"

She laughs. "You are very clever, Ilse," she says. "Of course we are afraid of the pemudas, but I think we will be able to see them before they see us, and we can hide."

It is true, we are on higher ground, and the jungle forest gives us plenty of places to hide at the side of the road.

"And we have turned toward Oro-oro Ombo," she says. "We are headed toward the Soember Brantas."

"How do you know, Tante?" Marijke asks. A little cheeky, I think, but Tante Zus laughs in the upward chiming tone that shows she is happy.

"I had some help from our old friend back at the désa," she says. "Surabaya is that way," she points to the east, "and Oro-oro Ombo is that way." She points south, in the direction of the mountains. "But we will have to leave this good road soon. It goes to Surabaya, and we do not want to go there."

Surabaya! Where we lived when the Japanese first came! I am excited.

"But Tante Zus! Our house is in Surabaya! Maybe Pap is there! Oh, let's go to Surabaya!"

"No, my darling," she says. "It is too dangerous. They are at war in Surabaya."

I am fearful for Pap, but I don't say anything in front of the children. Why worry them? Tante Zus stands and picks up the gunnysack. I am hopeful, but she does not open it.

No snack.

"Come, my loves," she says. "On to Oro-oro Ombo!"

We watch the sun chase away the pink dawn with a quick swipe, and soon the road takes a left turn to Surabaya. How can Surabaya be at war? It used to be my home. I think of the wide verandah and the hibiscus dolls Marijke and I fashioned. I feel like crying when we take the other road that leads us upward, into the mountains.

The new road is narrower. It feels safer, with a wall of trees and jungle growth on both sides where we can scurry if we need to hide. René needs to go peepee, so we all stop.

We all relieve ourselves, and when we are finished, Tante Zus calls us to a tiny circle surrounded by sword ferns. When we sit down, we are hidden from the road. She opens the gunnysack.

"How about some water?"

She must have seen my disappointment, because next, she says, "—and some pisang goreng?" Hurray!

We each drink from the jar, and then she unfolds one of the banana leaf packets. We are allowed to select our own piece of pisang goreng. René dives in first, then Marijke. I get a lovely fat piece, bigger than the others. I am glad I waited, politely. Tante Zus gives one to Edith and takes one for herself. There are still plenty, but one each is enough for now. We don't want to eat them all at once!

Back on the road, with no sign of a désa, we can talk as we go along. The sun is rising higher, but so is the road, so it is not as hot as before.

"We used to take vacations to visit Tante Annie and Oom Theo when it was hot," I tell Tante Zus

"Yes, it is always cooler in the Soember Brantas," she says. "And we should be coming upon the Brantas River soon."

Oh, yes! We will be able to soak ourselves in the water, and maybe even swim. I love to swim. I earned all of my swimming certificates at school before I was eight years old. Mam and Pap were proud. Oh, Mam. My breath catches in my throat, the way it always does when I am reminded she is gone and I will never see her again. And Pap, where are you? I get past the catch with a gasping sob, and then I let it all out with a noisy sigh, and at that very moment we see the white tunics coming toward us on the road ahead. These must be pemudas, lots of them, carrying bamboo spears, laughing and talking loudly.

It is too late to jump into the forest. They have seen us.

"Ilse, as they come closer, tell me a story in Pasar Maleis," Tante Zus whispers.

I hope the children remember to pretend we are natives on our way to our désa. I start talking about the delicious pisang goreng our grandmother packed for our journey, and about the delicious dinner she cooked for us last night. We move over to the side of the road, to let them pass, and they do not seem to pay much attention to us as they go by, close enough to reach out and touch them. My heart is pounding so hard in my head I am having trouble seeing clearly. They make some rude remarks about my aunt's skinny chest and legs, and they say they have seen monkeys in the jungle better looking than she. Tante Zus may not be able to speak their language very well, but she understands it and I hope her feelings are not hurt. We all keep our eyes on the dirt road, except for René who can't stop staring at the pemudas. When they have passed, I tell her in Pasar Maleis that I will be glad to get home so we can tell Father all about our visit. They might still be able to hear, so I add that Father will be happy when he sees Grandmother's tempeh and fried rice.

It worked. We keep walking, and we hear their voices getting farther away.

"Keep walking, darlings," Tante Zus whispers. "Do not turn around again, René."

My head is beginning to clear, and then I hear laughter behind us. I am too scared to turn around, but René does. "Here they come again!" he shouts.

Yes, I can see from the corner of my eye, they have come back. Some walk around in front of us, bringing us to a halt. They make a circle around us. It is like being surrounded by a prison fence again, only this fence wears stark-white pants and tunics.

"Ha!" says one of them in Pasar Maleis. "They think we cannot tell what they are."

"They look worse than bitch dogs," says another. "Our women would be ashamed of such an appearance." Everyone laughs.

They continue to make fun of us for thinking we could pass as natives. Then one takes the gunnysack and hands out the precious gifts to the others. They tear open the banana leaves, eating some of the food and throwing the rest into the underbrush. It is all I can do to keep from going after it. How I wish we had eaten all of the fried bananas at once. The tears begin to flow, as much for the lost pisang goreng as for the fact we have just been captured by freedom fighters who hate us and want to kill us.

The pemudas take us deep into the jungle forest, pushing, prodding, touching us in a familiar manner that makes me shudder. We make our way along a narrow footpath to a small clearing with only a few small huts—probably one of those camps the old grandmother warned us about. They throw us into a tiny bamboo hut, more of a cell. It has no windows, and air and light come in only through a barred gap—perhaps eighteen inches high—at the bottom of the door. The stink is terrible—feces, worse than the squatting holes ever were. Then

I realize we are not alone. Four women are already here. It is their waste I smell.

The pemudas make sport of tormenting us. We are dogs. They stand outside the hut and make jokes about what they are going to do to the dogs, and they throw food through the gap in the door. Dog food, they say. It doesn't matter what kind of food, for I am too terrified to eat.

They sharpen their machetes against a honing stone right in front of the opening in the bottom of the door. We can see the gleaming blades. Then they say, loudly enough for us to hear, that they will come for two of us at noon tomorrow, to cut off our heads. They talk about the best ways to chop off a head. They sit down outside the foul hut to smoke cigarettes and tell stories of the many decapitations they have performed. They loudly debate which two of us they will choose, and what they might do to us before they get around to killing us. Finally the tormenting stops and they leave.

The night hours pass, and over and over, I imagine the machete slicing through my neck—or Tante Zus's, or Marijke's, or the little ones'. I pray until I can't pray any more—to God, to Jesus, to Mam, to Pap if he is already in heaven.

Morning light comes in through the barred opening at the bottom of the door. But the pemudas do not come. They do not come! The sun passes over the hut, and they have not yet taken two of us out to behead. We do not see them all day long. Thank you, God. Perhaps they're gone.

But no—they gather again when the light begins to fade and the hut is dark inside. This time they say that beheading is too much trouble—they would have to clean their blades again as well as dispose of the bodies. So they decide to burn us alive instead, at noon tomorrow. They joke about flesh melting and how it smells, and how easy it will be to clean up the dogs' ashes when it is all over. Again, we wait. All night, all morning, and I imagine what it is going to feel like to melt into flames, and I wonder how much agonizing pain there will be before I actually die. I hope the flames will set the forest on fire and they will perish as well. And again, I pray.

When the sun is high and the light bright under the door, they return, still joking, always joking about our anguish and impending doom. Then, swoosh, a stream of kerosene, or perhaps gasoline gushes in under the door. We all scream, and nine of us are backed up against the wall opposite the door, knowing the liquid is about to be ignited. I step forward and Tante Zus tries to pull me back, screaming my name. I put my fingers in the liquid and bring them to my nose. No odor. Water. It is water!

We all cry and hold each other, and the pemudas laugh harder than ever. They leave with promises they will be back early in the morning to kill us all, for we are no longer fun to play with. I know this time they mean it, and I don't dare sleep away my last hours on earth, except in little short naps.

The clearing is strangely quiet as the early sun again lays down its light under our door. We hear none of the usual morning chatter out in the camp. Inside the reeking hut, no one talks. What do you say when you know you are about to die? Two of the women whisper to each other, but softly. The children and I huddle against Tante Zus, each of us taking turns crying. And of course, there is the praying.

Again, we wait. But again, no one comes. We see no movement through our narrow view of the encampment. Then, a miracle. Soldiers appear—Gurkhas! Those East Indians who belong to the British Army and wear turbans instead of caps or helmets. We all begin to shout.

While the Gurkhas knock the lock off our reeking jail, we hug each other and weep with as much, and maybe more force than we had wept when we thought we were about to die. I guess the relief and the gratitude that comes of being delivered from the angel of death just gushes out. Anyway, we can't control it.

The Gurkhas stand back and stare at us as we tumble out of the filth of the hut. They must be shocked and disgusted to find us covered in our own and each other's piss and shit. They do not ask how we happen to be here, but they tell us that if we have anyplace to go, we must go there as quickly as possible.

"Get away from this place," says one. "You are not safe here." As if we need to be told that!

We flee as fast as a woman and four children can flee through the tropical jungle. I have no doubt that we were scheduled to die this morning. I thank God for the Gurkhas. Thank you, thank you, thank you.

I do not know, and I do not care where the four women went. We came that close to dying together, and I never even learned their names.

Chapter 26.
Clean Sheets and Tobacco Tea

Brutality was not limited to the Indonesian side of the war for independence. Raymond "Turk" Westerling, commander of a special unit of the Dutch army, was notorious for his ruthless slaughter of native islanders suspected of being freedom fighters or of harboring them. They say he and his murderous thugs—many of them Indonesians from Maluku—were responsible for as many as 5,000 civilian deaths and were accused of committing atrocities against children and hospital patients.

These monstrous Westerlings, as they were called, connect with my story in a memory that rises, unbidden, to my mind's eye. I have spent a lifetime trying to rid myself of it, but all I have managed to erase are the details of where and when it happened. I believe it took place along the Brantas River as we continued on to Oro-oro Ombo from the pemuda outpost.

We are so cautious. Now that we have found the road that will take us further into the mountains toward Oro-oro Ombo, we do not talk at all. We do not want to miss any sound that might be pemudas. Every time a tree scrapes against another or a rodent rustles in the brush, we dive for the side of the road and burrow under anything that will hide us.

At last, we find the Brantas River where we can drink our fill and wash off at least some of the foulness, but without soap it is hard to get all the way down to the skin. We lower our heads in the moving waters to unload some lice. The nits, of course, stay put.

When we come upon *fijvers*—small ponds—we stuff ourselves with the delicious fruit from the *tjiplukan* vines that grow along the edges of the moist banks. When we are really lucky, we find *belimbing*—starfruit—growing on small trees in the wild. Not tempeh and pisang goreng, but adequate to keep the hunger from hurting and from occupying my mind every waking moment. Besides, the thought of pisang goreng brings an image of pemudas tearing open our food packages. Any image of pemudas strikes my gut with panic that stops my breath as well as my appetite.

The river takes twists and turns, but the road keeps a southeasterly bearing. We spy the occasional snake, but we know which ones to stay away from and the others don't bother us. I am always glad to see the river, and I leave the road to walk along the bank every chance I get. It is like home to me until I round a bend and see fingers of red water reaching out into the current from a pool on the other side of the river.

Something is not right, and I drop down to hide in the thick grass that edges the bank. I see a big white building across the river—a hospital? an orphanage? I see two soldiers carrying little children who are limp in their arms, down to the riverbank. More soldiers are coming along behind them, also carrying limp little children across the green lawn between the building and the river. When the first two get to the water they drop those babies onto the ground and pull machetes out of their scabbards.

As the blades swing down, my stomach lurches with a spasm that rolls into my throat and stops my scream, and I curl forward into a ball. I hear two splashes, and then two more, and I know why the pool is red. I clench my eyes and my jaws tight, but I cannot close my ears to what is going on. Why aren't the little ones screaming? They must already be dead, or perhaps they have been knocked unconscious. Oh God, God, please make it stop. Oh, God, please, please, please. I dare not move or make a sound.

When the sounds stop, I lift my head and only the dead children are there, in the pool, dark red near the bank, little heads separated from little bodies. The soldiers have gone. I crawl through the heavy grass and the brush to the road. I stand and take deep breaths until my legs will carry me down the road to find Tante Zus and the children.

"Where have you been, Ilse?" my aunt scolds. "We have been waiting for you for a long time. I was afraid you had fallen into the river and drowned."

I can't tell them what I have just seen. I can't talk at all. Maybe later, when Tante Zus and I are alone. But I ask, in a whisper, if we can walk faster, and I promise not to walk along the riverbank again. Between the pemuda jail and what I just saw, I know that I live in a world gone mad. Will I go mad, as well?

When we stop to sleep, I cannot close my eyes over the sight of those babies and the red pool. My own little sisters and my little brother are sound asleep, safe for now. But I imagine them in the arms of those soldiers, and I cannot stand it any longer. I stand up and go to my aunt. She is on her side, her back to me, and I lean over her.

"Tante Zus," I whisper, and she rolls onto her back. I don't know if she has been asleep. "I have to tell you something."

I pull her away from the little ones. They must not hear my story. We sit down on a low hill and I tell her about the red pool. Partway through the telling, I begin to shake. I cannot let the screams come out, so I hold my breath and rock back and forth until each scream passes, and then I shake some more and tell some more. When it is finished, I am in my tante's arms. She is sobbing, too, and she pets me until I am quiet, at last. When we go back to the little ones, I lie on my side, against Tante Zus. I have never felt so exhausted, and I close my eyes.

By the time the sun is part-way up the sky and we have climbed a long way up a mountain, our road leads us into a small town, and I begin to see things that seem familiar. Is this Oro-oro Ombo, at last? Tante Zus turns onto a road that follows the curve of the mountain, and then I see it—Tante Annie's bamboo bungalow off to the right, down its own lane.

"Tante Zus, Tante Zus—" I am so excited, I can only point. The house is exactly as I remember it: one story, made of bamboo. It is built high enough off the ground to keep the water from entering during the rainy season. The porch is wide, covered with a slanting roof for shade. As we turn into the lane, however, I see something that is not as I remember. Marijke asks first.

"Tante, is that an ape?"

We all stop part way up the lane, to stare at an orangutan that is chained to a stake beside the porch. The ape stares back and tilts its head to examine us closely. He looks more curious than mean, but I am not sure I want to go forward. Tante Zus is just as perplexed as I, but she finally picks up René—I already have Edith on my back—and she gives Marijke and me a little nudge.

"He is chained. He won't be able to reach us," she says.

I am not so sure. It looks like a long chain. I walk to the steps, never taking my eyes off that ape.

When we step onto the porch, the door bursts open and Tante Annie and Oom Theo are upon us, hugging us and crying.

"Zus, Zus, is it really you?"

"Ilse, my darling, you are already a woman!"

"Marijke, little one, you have grown so!"

"René, you were a baby when we saw you last!"

"And this, we have never seen this little one." Edith was born after our last visit.

And then, they realize that some are missing.

"But where is Henk?"

"Where is Mies?"

Tante Zus explains that we have not seen Pap since he left De Hotel and have no idea whether he is alive or not. It is not good news to tell his sister. Tante Annie looks sad and shakes her head.

"And Mies?" she asks.

"We lost our darling Mies at Camp Halmaheira, God rest her dear soul."

Tante Annie breathes in, hard, and she sucks her lips in and then purses them out, but the tears spill over anyway. She wipes them away with her hand and squeezes the bridge of her nose. I know she loved my mother. Everyone loved my mother. When she can speak, Tante Annie pushes the door open and waves us in.

"Come in, come in, my schatjes. You are so thin, we must remedy that!"

I put Edith down and she shuffles up to Tante Annie. I wait, to take one more look at the orangutan who has been watching us from the yard. Oom Theo waits behind me.

"That is our attack monkey," he says, laughing. But I can tell he does not think it is funny. I wonder what an attack monkey does, but now there are other things to ask about.

"Where is Eddie?" I ask Oom Theo. I am surprised to see his face turn hard, like he is trying to avoid something he does not want to deal with.

"Edwina is in Batavia with her brother and sister," he says. "At the Salvation Army School."

"Oh, so far away," I say, disappointed. My cousin Eddie and I are the same age, and I remember the fun we used to have together. Perhaps she will want to come home on a visit when she hears we are here. But not until I get clean. She would not want to come near me now.

Our relatives have a most interesting water system. Water travels from the mountains in open bamboo troughs. You can see these open "pipes" propped up across the fields, and one leads right up to a great cement tank just off the porch of the house. I peek in and see that water is trickling into the tank. It never stops. During the dry season, it is a slow stream, like now. During the rainy season, I remember, it gushes into the tank which overflows all over the ground when the water is not used fast enough. Another pipe carries water into the kitchen, where it drips out into a sink. But the water used for bathing and cleaning is carried in buckets. Right now I am anxious to fill the mandi bak behind the house and start the bathing. Today we will need the tub!

We soak and scrub ourselves clean. Tante Zus and I help the younger ones, all of us naked, all of us reveling in the joy of soap and water. Our bodies gleam pink with the vigorous scrubbing of our soap-filled bath mitts, the *washandjes* I used to take for granted. Now they are a luxury. I cannot get enough of hair washing. Tante Annie gives us some special blue soap which we use for our hair even though it stings the sores and makes the little ones cry. Tante Annie finds clothing for us, and the ragged, wretched jumpsuits we arrived in are thrown onto a burn pile. Good riddance.

At dinnertime we sit around the table and eat by the light of the gas pump-lamp that stands in the center. No electricity. My relatives live simply, but they live well and eat well—dried fish fried in hot oil; kangkung, the seasoned spinachy dish; berang, a spicy eggplant dish, more than we can eat. I can hardly bear to break away from the comfort of the kitchen, real chairs, food at the end of my arm's reach, safety. But eventually I say goodnight and go into Eddie's room where the children are already sleeping on *bali balis*—bamboo cots with thick, comfortable mattresses. The bloody pool still crouches in the corner of my mind, but I think I will be able to sleep this night. Thank you, thank you, thank you, I say as I slide into Eddie's bali bali, between clean sheets.

I am sorry to say we will need more than blue soap to conquer the head lice.

"Theo," Tante Annie calls, "you must go to the warong to buy tobacco—lots of it." I remember the warong down the road where Eddie and I were allowed to go for shaved ice treats. It was not much more than a big trailer with an open window where you placed your order under a canvas awning, but we felt very important when we went there. The warong is handy for Tante Annie and Oom Theo and saves them the trouble of going into town, except for big purchases. They say Oro-oro Ombo is not very safe now.

Oom Theo rolls his own cigarettes, but I am curious about why he needs <u>lots</u> of tobacco today.

"You will find out," says Tante Annie, and she and Tante Zus start to laugh. I am already not sure I want to find out.

While Oom Theo is gone, Tante Annie gives a large pair of scissors to Tante Zus who calls us out to the porch. "Come, Ilse," she says. "You must set the example for the others."

I sit on a stool and Tante Zus cuts off my hair, whack, whack, whack. She and Tante Annie bend to look at me, first one way and then another. "A little more here," says one. "How about a little more there?" says the other. When they are satisfied they have it right, they tell me to sweep up the mound of hair, put it into a paper bag and take it to the burn pile. It will stink when it burns, but I smile to think of all the lice that will go up in flames. Then I shudder to recall how close we came, back at the pemuda camp—no, I cannot let myself think of it.

"Come, Marijke," says Tante Zus, patting the seat of the stool.

Between broom sweeps, my hands find their way to my head. My hair has never been this short. I wonder what I look like, so when I have delivered the bag to the burn pile, I go into the house to find a mirror. I am not sure how I like it. I try to pull it back to make a kondah, but it doesn't work—there is not enough hair to make a bun. Oh, well, it will grow. I go back out to the porch to watch the rest of the shearings. They get as close to René's scalp as they can. Poor little boy, we can see the sores all over his head.

Then I find out what the tobacco is for. Tante Annie builds a fire in the outdoor anglo and puts a lot of water in a big pot with the tobacco. It smells foul as it begins to boil. She tells us it is tobacco tea

"Do we have to drink it?" cries René, and I think my aunts are going to fall over from laughing so hard.

"No, my pet," says one of them when the laughing fit is over. "Just wait—you shall see."

When the tobacco tea has cooled, I am the first one to see.

Each of us gets a thorough tobacco shampoo. Oh, how it stinks, and it stings the sores until they burn. We beg, but the aunts will not let us rinse the foul stuff off our heads. By the time it dries it does not hurt any more.

"Oh, let's play Kill the Lice!" Marijke says. We have to explain the game to our aunts who think it is a fine idea. Tante Annie brings us a sisir-sirit and an old ripped-up sheet to put between us. As we bend over the sheet, the lice begin to fall out of our hair, but we do not have to chase them down. They are dead. When we run the comb through our short locks, hundreds more fall out, and the nits, too. We dance around the sheet, combing every strand of hair and watching the vermin fall.

At night, after our bellies have been filled and our family has sat around the lamplight to share stories—good stories of old times together—it is a pleasure to go to bed. We are free of head lice for the first time in years, thanks to Tante Annie's tobacco tea.

Looking back, it was nothing short of a miracle that we made it to the Soember Brantas and Tante Annie's. I have no way of knowing how many miles we walked, as our route took us "as the crow flies" through hostile back country, most of it during drought, all of it under threat of being captured by those who wanted us dead. All this without shoes, without directions, and much of the time without food.

Unwelcome images still come to me in nightmares that tear my slumber into shreds and keep me awake until dawn. Sometimes it is the pemuda hut. Sometimes it is the bloody pool. If that pool was not filled by Westerlings, then I am sure it was filled by his disciples, and they and he should be rotting in Hell. I understand that many of his "troops" were later tried as war criminals. Westerling himself fled Indonesia under a fake passport and returned to the Netherlands where he lived a comfortable life until 1989. Hailed as a hero by some Dutch patriots, he was never returned to Indonesia to stand trial.

How could anyone think he was a hero?

Chapter 27.
White Tunics and Poisoned Spears

The Indonesian revolutionaries and the Netherlands were at war, a shooting war between armies. But in the Soember Brantas it was a war conducted with spears and machetes and drums. White-clad pemudas traveled along the road in noisy gangs, but they showed no interest in our little bamboo bungalow at the end of the lane. We knew that could change at any moment. Drums pounded out their coded messages every night, reminding us we were under siege. But anxiety can be softened by everyday comforts, especially when you have been without those comforts for a long time. We had plenty to eat, we slept in clean beds free of vermin, and we got new clothes. Life was good at Tante Annie's.

⚜

Tante Zus is busy on the sewing machine. René, Edith and Marijke already have their new clothes—dresses for the girls and short pants and a shirt for René. Now it is my turn. The fabric is bright and cheerful. Tante Annie bought it to make things for her own children, but that was before she knew they would be leaving. I guess she does not plan to visit them and take new clothing. Batavia is on the far western side of Java; Oro-oro Ombo is on the eastern side.

We got to choose our own colors. I chose a print of yellow stars on a deep blue background because it reminds me of our first night of freedom when I connected the stars to make pictures. At night I still like to go out and make pictures and think of Mam, but not when the drums are beating. I hate the drums.

My dress will be finished soon. Tante Zus is attaching a yellow ruffle around the bottom. Marijke wants me to come outside and play gotrik. I don't know why—I can always hit the puck farther than she can, although she is getting so good she will probably beat me one of these days. Usually we spend the morning playing outside, but this morning I am more interested in trying on my dress the minute it is finished. Marijke is disappointed.

"Why don't you bring the paper and the colored pencils," I suggest. "We can draw pictures."

I draw the outline of another butterfly. I love to design the wings and fill them in with lovely color combinations. Marijke draws a scribbling design with the magenta pencil. She will fill in the scribble-spaces with different colors and I will tell her it is beautiful. She will do five scribble pictures before I finish one butterfly. It must be perfect. I could win prizes with my butterflies.

I have barely put the finishing touches on the wing design when Tante Zus holds up my dress.

"Put it on, Ilse, let's see how it looks," she says.

I love it and I twirl, letting the ruffle wrap around my legs, first one way and then the other as I change directions. I am dancing! Tante Zus is happy. Tante Annie comes in to share the fun of a brand new dress with a yellow ruffle. She carries a basket full of laundry that has been drying on the hibiscus bushes out beyond the laundry tubs in the back yard. I bury my head in one of the thick towels and breath in the sunshine fragrance. I have finally gotten the stink of that pemuda jail out of my nostrils.

Marijke and I go outside to find our gotrik sticks. We will finish our pictures after lunch when we will want to stay in out of the heat.

The midday meal is the big meal of the day. Tante Annie and Tante Zus have prepared it together, as usual. I am every day grateful that I do not have to find food for the family. As a matter of fact, I do not have to do much of anything. The aunties take care of all the chores, and they keep Edith and René occupied. That is just fine with me. One thing interferes with my happiness, however.

My aunts insist that we learn how to use eating utensils again. It is so much easier to turn the four fingers of my eating hand into a scoop, dip out a clump of rice, top it with a side dish, and then push it into my mouth with my thumb. It is how we have eaten since we left De Hotel, and it is how I like to eat. But the aunts say no, it is not civilized and we must be civilized. We must all use knives and forks and spoons for at least five minutes at each meal before they will let us eat the sensible way. Eventually, they say, we will have to give up using our fingers altogether.

"Quit dawdling, Ilse," Tante Annie says. She frowns at me. She knows I am wasting time until the five minutes are up. I pick up my fork and wave it around a few times and everybody laughs. I put in my five minutes and then go back to scooping and shoving.

While Tante Annie and Tante Zus clean up after the meal, Marijke and I walk with Oom Theo to the warong to get the daily newspaper. We can never leave the cottage without the company of an adult. We do not even go out in the yard unless Oom Theo or one of the aunts is outside with us. When we return, I have time to finish my butterfly before the mid-dag dutje, and Marijke gives up scribble designs for flower gardens. They are really quite nice. She may take after Pap as an artist. We both like lively colors.

After the nap, we take old newspapers out to the porch and create sculptures with them—birds, fish, houses. I have enjoyed relearning paper folding a great deal more than relearning the use of spoons and forks. The orangutan looks on with interest, and we talk to him just to be sociable. I still would not want to get anywhere near the end of that chain, though.

After the evening meal Tante Zus puts the two little ones to bed and hears their prayers. We all visit around the pump-lamp at the table, and finally Marijke takes herself off to bed. I stay and listen to the adults talk about old times until my eyes begin to droop, and finally I leave the circle to go to the mandi bak.

The full moon is so bright I need no candlelight to bathe and put on my pajamas—well, my cousin's pajamas, on loan. Back in our bedroom, I fold my new dress carefully and lay it across the end of the bed. Then I say my prayers. Thank you, thank you, thank you, and please take care of Pap, wherever he is, and please tell Mam I love her and wish she were here. The moon is centered in the windowpane, and I must look away after a moment; its glow makes my eyes throb.

I hear shouting. Have I been asleep? I don't think so, but the moon is no longer framed in the center of my window. The noise that brought me fully awake is getting louder—shouting voices—and I hear the ape screeching. I am paralyzed for the moment. It must be pemudas. I throw my new dress on over my pajamas. By now René and Marijke are awake. Thank heaven Edith is still asleep. I feel that old sense of responsibility for my brother and sisters, and I am afraid.

"Stay here, do you hear me? Stay here," I tell them. I leave no doubt that they must mind me, just like the days in Camp Halmaheira. They are crying, but quietly, as I leave the room.

My uncle is already standing at the door, fully dressed. My aunts are behind him. They do not know I am here. Through the window, I see many men walking up the lane. Their tunics almost glow in the moonlight, they are so white. Each man carries a long bamboo spear. The ape is jumping up and down, "Hoo, hoo, hoo, scree, scree, scree." He is agitated. The men stop before they get to the porch.

"Shut this ape up, old man, or he will be on the end of my spear," says one, a very young man, perhaps only a few years older than I.

My uncle steps onto the porch to quiet the orangutan. I see that he is holding his hunting knife behind his back. My aunts move up to the door. They have their arms around each other.

"What do you want, my friends?" How can my uncle be so calm, so brave, with pemudas at his front door?

"We are not your friends, Theo Gerrits," says the leader, "but we have decided to do you a favor."

"And what is that, Martukosumo?" My uncle knows this man! Perhaps he has worked for Oom Theo on the plantation.

"We have decided to give you warning. We have let you stay here much too long, but you have been fair to many of us and helped us with our debts."

Oom Theo's shoulders relax a little and his grip shifts a bit on the knife handle.

"But we can not let you stay here any longer. Tomorrow night many of our brothers will be joining us from other villages, and if you are here we will come back to kill all of you. They will be here by nightfall. You have that long to save your lives and get out."

"Thank you, Martukosumo. You and your father have been good friends—" Oom Theo begins, but the crowd starts up with some kind of chatter, and some shake their spears.

"Do not call me 'friend' unless you want to end it right here." Martukosumo sounds like a snarling animal. "Just be gone tomorrow."

He turns and waves his spear toward the road. They all turn and walk back down the lane, their backs shimmering in the moonlight. I can breathe again, but the stench of the pemuda hut in the jungle is back in my nostrils. The adults know I am here, but they pay no attention to me. They begin to make plans. I head back for the bedroom to comfort the children. There will be no sleep this night.

Oom Theo and the women move quickly. It is just like the day the Japanese ordered us out of our home in Surabaya, only this time René has no teddy bear and we have no servants to help. And we have no place to go.

Many years later I learned the real purpose of the attack orangutan. My uncle kept a sharp hunting knife under his belt at all times. It was the knife I saw in his hand the night of the pemudas' visit. He was prepared, I learned, to slit the throats of his loved ones before he would let them be taken by the monsters in white. The attack orangutan was there to give him time to do it. Thankfully, that never came to pass.

Chapter 28.
Return of the Gurkhas

According to my calculations, we must have left Oro-oro Ombo in mid-to-late October of 1945. Rumor had it that a hotel in one of the cities was taking in refugees, so that's where we headed. It might have been Malang; it might have been Surabaya. At the time it didn't matter to me; I just followed Oom Theo's lead.

According to my historical timeline, we couldn't have picked a worse time to walk into an East Javan city. Upper East Java, especially Surabaya, was being torn apart by Dutch and Gurkha troops battling the Indonesian Republican Army, who had the edge with Japanese tanks. The Indonesian Republicans were either murdering or throwing Dutch and Indies civilians into prison. We were on our way into a reign of terror, but we didn't know that when we struck out on our three-, maybe four-day journey.

By noon we are on the road, on foot. Midday is not a good time to be traveling, but the sooner we get away from the bamboo cottage, the better. Oom Theo's last act in Oro-oro Ombo is to deliver the orangutan to one of his farm hands.

I am rather sorry to see the orangutan left behind. He has been entertaining.

This is certainly an improvement over my last journey on foot. This time we each carry well-organized gunny-sack packs of food and clothing, and water is plentiful in brooks and streams. No more dry season. We have sandals on our feet, and we can walk on the road. No sense trying to hide—at least a hundred of us are walking out of Oro-oro Ombo. If we were not homeless, and if we were not under attack by these Indonesians who used to be our friends, the hike might seem more like a Soember Brantas camping vacation.

As we near the city, it becomes obvious this is no vacation. Crowds of frantic people are leaving. We hear gunfire and artillery exploding somewhere in the distance. It does not seem like a very good place to be, but Oom Theo is determined, and at last we arrive at a large hotel packed full of displaced people. I am reminded of De Hotel.

The hotel is all noise and screaming people looking for other screaming people. We have no one to look for, so we stay quiet, glued to Tante Zus. I look around and see that most of the "guests" seem to be Hollanders, but I see some Indies, too, like us. Somehow, Oom Theo gets room assignments for us. Tante Zus, Marijke, René, Edith and I are in one wing; Oom Theo and Tante Annie in another.

We elbow our way through the crowds until we find our room, and when we get there, what do we find? Mattresses on the floor, just like Halmaheira. Marijke and I look at each other and drop down to inspect one of the mattresses. Thank heaven, no bedbugs. Tante Zus closes the door on the noise outside, and the tiny room is peaceful.

When we leave the room at dinnertime, we are back in the chaos. Everybody talks at once, trying to make themselves heard over the din. Rumors bounce all around us. The Republican army is bringing in a tank to blow up the hotel! We are about to be evicted from the premises! The Dutch East Indies Army is very near! The Dutch East Indies Army has been annihilated by the Republican Army! The hotel is about to become a prison! The Gurkhas are coming to take us to a safe place! It is all very confusing. All we can do, I think, is wait to see which of the rumors is true. In the meantime, the mattresses are clean and the food is good, although you have to wait a long time for it.

"They're coming," we keep hearing on our third morning at the hotel. Someone even knocks on our door and calls, "They're coming!"

Who's coming? The good army? The bad army? The Gurkhas? The pemudas? Finally curiosity gets the best of Tante Zus. She picks up René.

"Get Edith, Ilse. Marijke, hang onto my arm. We are going outside."

We walk by Tante Annie's room. The door is wide open, but Tante Annie and Oom Theo are not there. We do not see any of their belongings, either. I can see that Tante Zus is puzzled. We push through crowds of people to get to the hotel verandah. It is even more crowded there, but we find a place to stand together by an iron railing that overlooks the driveway.

Soon we hear the roar of engines. Just like I remember at De Hotel, military trucks drive into the hotel compound and soldiers—dozens of them—get out of the trucks. But this time they are our friends, the Gurkhas, wearing their turbans.

"Be calm! Be calm!" they shout, and finally the crowd quiets down.

A Gurkha leader tells us that they have come to transport us to safety. The city is out of control, and anyone who stays will be in danger of being executed.

"But this is my home," calls out one old gentleman, a Dutchman. "What if I don't want to leave?"

The Gurkha shrugs. "You will probably die here," he answers. "We cannot protect you."

I hear a humming through the crowd, and an elderly lady nearby says, "I am too old to start all over."

Another says, "I will stay and take my chances."

Why would anyone want to take such a chance, I wonder, but I don't have much time to think about it. The Gurkhas are forming lines for people to get into the trucks. Many of the older folks are winding back through the crowd, away from the trucks and into the hotel lobby. The rest of the crowd seems determined to get on the first truck, but the Gurkhas insist upon keeping order, and the lines get organized. There is some noise—children crying, parents yelling as they try to keep their families together, but no one is pushing or shoving any more.

We are not in a line. We don't even have our belongings with us.

"Tante Zus," I say, tugging at her arm. I think we should be hurrying to get our things and get on a truck, but she is not in a hurry. And now she has someone to look for—Tante Annie and Oom Theo. I am alarmed that the trucks will leave without us.

"Yes, yes, Ilse," she says, and she herds us back into the hotel. It is much less crowded now, but there are still people in the halls. Some are hugging and kissing goodbye, and we hear people begging the old folks to come along, to get on the trucks and leave the hotel.

We get to our room to pick up our packs, and back down the hall we go. Many people are crying, and the old people are congregating in the hotel lobby. They are lining up at the windows. That's when we see Tante Annie and Oom Theo.

"Come," yells Tante Zus, waving at them to join us. They are carrying their bags, too, but they are waving and yelling, "Goodbye!"

"Goodbye?" I shout. "Aren't you coming with us?" But no one hears me, and Tante Zus pushes me toward the door. I wave at my aunt and uncle as I start down the steps. It is the best I can do. The trucks are not going to wait much longer.

Most of the trucks are full, their tailgates locked into place. I have sudden panic that there is no more room, especially when I see people in the trucks pulling others in over the tops of the tailgates. Tante Zus is not at all panicky, and we line up behind people who are beginning to push and shove again. I guess they are also afraid the trucks will run out of room. We do not push, and finally we get into the very last truck carrying passengers. I throw a sack onto the floorboards of a truck and climb in after it. This feels so familiar. But this time I get to sit on a bench. Hurray!

The gate of our truck clangs into place. Then we hear engines start up, one by one, and the line of trucks begins to move. Some of the people in our truck are weeping loudly. I cannot imagine why anyone would be sad to leave this place, especially when someone is on the way to execute us. Then I look out the back of the truck and I see, in the windows of the hotel, the old people waving.

Only then does it really sink into my mind that these people will be dead soon—they have chosen to face the executioners. I catch my breath in a gasp—Tante Annie and Oom Theo! But no, they are not old. And they were dressed for travel, with their bags. Surely they are not staying behind. But where are they?

We are in a long line of very slow-moving trucks—a convoy—maybe fifteen, maybe more. I try to count them as we go around curves and I can see what's ahead of us. The first truck is full of soldiers, and the last truck—the one behind us— is full of soldiers. We are book-ended by soldiers! Soldiers also walk along beside us, looking very alert with their rifles in their hands ready to fire, not slung across their backs.

The word drifts down to us. We are going to the city of Ambarawa, near Semarang, to Fort Willem II, an old penitentiary in Central Java. This is too much to comprehend. After all we have been through since we walked out of Camp Hamaheira, we are going back to a prison no more than thirty miles from there? I want to cry, but I remind myself we are under protection this time of people who are on our side and want to keep us safe. They have already saved our lives once.

The convoy rumbles along until we are out of the city. The Gurkhas climb into the trucks, and we move a little faster. My head tips forward and I am snoozing when I hear—

Ping! Ping! Ping!

Our Gurkhas yell "Down! Down!" as they leap out of the truck. Everyone falls forward, onto the floor, and we hear rifles firing right beside us. It is our Gurkhas returning fire at the snipers who are shooting at us. The shooting stops and we all climb back into our seats. We are shaky, and some of us were almost squashed, but we are all okay.

The line starts moving again, but the Gurkhas are again walking beside the truck. They are taking no chances, I guess. The danger is past, but not as far as Tante Zus is concerned.

"Down," she says to the four of us. "Down on the floor!"

"Tante Zus— " we begin to complain, even Edith. It is hot and dirty on the floor of the truck.

"Hush! Not a word," she warns. "The bullets will not find you so easily if you are flat on the floor."

"Then Tante Zus, you must get down here with us," I say, and I am not being sassy. I do not want the bullets to find her either.

"Nonsense. There is not room for everyone on the floor," she says. Family by family, all the children are sent to the floor.

"Lie flat," our aunt commands, and everyone lies flat. It is very uncomfortable for anything but sleeping, and we make that easier by using each other's bodies for pillows. My head rests on the stomach of a little boy whose mother cries all the time. There is a lot of crying in the truck. When some stop, others begin.

We travel in great discomfort and fear. The prospect of ambush or attack seems to lie around every corner. The adults will not budge on our travel positions, so the only times we are allowed to get up off the floor are when the convoy veers off the road into the protection of the woods for bathroom breaks or meals. Not that I can eat very much. For the second time in my life, my fear replaces my hunger.

I hate being at the end of the convoy. It seems all of the fumes funnel into our truck and come to rest at floor level. Why couldn't Tante Zus have been a little quicker and gotten us up front?

We have been traveling through the woods, big trees shading us from the sun, so the heat on the floor has not been unbearable for once. We are just coming out of the forest when I hear a familiar sound. An airplane. As always, I think of Bandung and Van Dorp's. The truck brakes screech, and all the people inside are thrown from their seats, landing on top of us. We hear machine gun fire at the same time the gate of our truck bangs down and one of the Gurkhas is yelling at us, "Get out! Get out! Run for the trees!" I jump from the truck right behind René. Where are the others?

"Run, run," I hear Tante Zus's voice among the many that are screaming the same thing, and so I put my head down and run. I hear other kinds of screaming, too. We are close to the trees, but people in the first trucks have a long way to run.

Another plane is coming toward us. Rat-a-tat-tat-tat-tat, the bullets spew out. People fall and the first truck, the one that carries Gurkhas, explodes. I see people on fire, and their screams are terrible. It is Van Dorp's all over again.

The planes are circling around. By now we are under the trees. Tante Zus and the girls have caught up with René and me. We throw ourselves face down in the grass. I raise my head enough to see another of our trucks hit and burst into flame. Metal flies everywhere, and some people are close enough to get hit by the fragments. Others are hit by bullets. People are screaming and dying.

The planes do not return, but they have done their damage. Tante Zus makes us stay under our tree while she goes to help the wounded. An awful smell hovers and stings my nostrils. I have never smelled it before, but I know it is flesh burning, and I am thrown back to the jungle jail for a flash of a moment.

I sit there with my sisters and my brother, all of us huddled together, and I thank God we were not in one of the trucks up front. Thank you, thank you, thank you.

Chapter 29.
Fort Willem II

Imagine the task of rescuing 400,000 men, women and children who have been displaced by one war, only to find themselves knee deep in another one. Most of the families had been separated, so add reuniting families to that task—families that were so scattered they had no idea whether their spouses, fathers, mothers, sons, or daughters were still living, let alone where they were living. Where do you start? One place to start was Fort Willem II, the historic penitentiary in Ambarawa which became a refugee camp for people like us.

Rolling into Fort Willem II, it is obvious that the only way in or out of this place is through the gate. I have never seen such walls. They are solid concrete, at least three stories high, topped like a brandgang wall with sparkling glass fragments. The gate—all iron grillwork, is wide enough for four big trucks to pass through side by side and room to spare. More impressive than anything we ever saw at Camp Halmaheira! But one thing Fort Willem II has in common with Camp Halmaheira—soldiers everywhere, with weapons. I think I have developed another phobia; I am almost paralyzed at the sight of a man in uniform.

Maybe it's from the Kempeitai. Maybe it's from that day on the Brantas River. No, I don't allow myself to think of that.

Our truck is the last to roll past a number of low buildings. They look like offices of some kind. Then we pass a grove of waringin trees, and they have a sea of tables under them. Finally we come to a stop in a large open area in front of one of the enormous, high, concrete buildings—the very biggest building I have ever seen.

René is the first one out of the truck, jumping off the end of the tailgate and landing on his feet. Isn't he the nimble one? I sit on the tailboard and then slide off, avoiding the hand of the Gurkha who is trying to help. Tante Zus thanks him for helping her with the sacks, and then he lifts Marijke and Edith to the ground. They don't seem to mind at all. I guess I am the only one with the phobia. He points back toward the buildings we just passed and says something to my aunt. Tante Zus nods. We pick up our gunny-bags, and she waves us all in the direction of the trees and the tables.

René and Marijke skip ahead of us, and Edith trots along behind them. I would like to skip, too, but it would be undignified for a 12-and-a-half-year-old, so I walk along beside Tante Zus. Hundreds of people are milling about, and the little ones weave in and out of the crowd. Tante Zus catches up with Edith and pulls her back to walk with us. René finally runs into a woman who is looking at a piece of paper and not watching where she is going. That puts a stop to the skipping.

"René, Marijke, mind your manners," says Tante Zus, and they rejoin us to walk the rest of the way.

We join the crowd of people passing time at the long wooden tables under the trees. We put our belongings in a cradle of tree roots and stand by them. We can sit down, but we choose to stand after all those hours on the floor of a truck.

"Wait for me here," Tante Zus tells us, and she walks off toward a building that has a sign, Check In Here. All the buildings have signs: Registration, Red Cross Message Center, Facilities, Prisoner Affairs, Laundry, Post Office. The biggest building says *Gaar Keuken*, the kitchen, and I see Dutch and Indies ladies working inside. I hope the Indies ladies do most of the cooking so the food will be spicy. I would like to explore, but Tante Zus said to stay here.

An Indies soldier in a Royal Dutch East Indies Army uniform—like the one Pap wore when he was in the KNIL—walks toward us. My muscles freeze. I watch the ground in front of him until he is standing directly in front of us. I raise my eyes but not my head. He is smiling. His hand swings forward and I cringe, but he is only offering a candy bar to Marijke.

"Young lady, would you like some chocolate?"

"Oh, yes!" She is very quick to take the candy. He reaches into the pouch that hangs at his side.

"How about some for your little brother and sister?"

Edith and René jump up and down. They are not a bit shy when it comes to chocolate.

"And the big sister?"

I would like to have some chocolate, only I would have to reach out toward this man and I cannot make myself move. I just shake my head.

"She likes chocolate," Marijke tells him. "She is just being a scaredy-cat." I frown at her for saying such a thing about me to a stranger. How does she know?

"Oh, that is too bad," he says, and he pats René's shoulder as he moves on to give away more chocolate.

The children are absorbed with getting the wrappers off the candy. I look around, to take stock of our new home. People pour in and out of the buildings. Some seem to be officials or workers, some are dressed like us, apparently as homeless as we are. Men and women wearing khaki uniforms with Red Cross patches sewn on their pockets and backs zig-zag between buildings. They also wear dark berets with a Red Cross patch sewn on the jaunty part in front. Everyone seems to have a purpose.

Children play beyond the tables, still under the umbrella of the huge waringins. Some are running around in a game of *krygertje,* trying to avoid being tagged by the little blond-haired boy who is "it." Several circles are playing *knickers*, and I wonder whatever happened to my beautiful glass marbles. I notice Marijke is watching the gotrik game going on out beyond the trees. But my favorite is *bikkelen.* My hand itches to toss up the little rubber ball and scoop up the sturdy copper bikkeles from the ground, first one, then two, then three at a time. Oh, yes, I am very good at bikkelen, and I want very much to play.

I hear Tante Zus. "Come, schatjes. We have a new home in that big old fortress." We pick up our packs and off we go.

Edith complains about her pack. "It's too heavy," she whines, and she drags it along in the dirt behind her. I am deciding between carrying the bag for her and telling her to stop complaining when a KNIL soldier swoops her up, sets her in the crook of his arm and tosses her bag over his shoulder.

"A tiring trip, eh, short stuff? I am Erik. What is your name?"

I halt and my jaw drops and locks open as I hear Edith giggle. "Ay-dith Eh-vuh-Layn Veere," she tells him, being very precise about the pronunciation.

"A beautiful name for a beautiful little girl," he says, and then he and Tante Zus visit while we walk. No one even slows down, except me. When I get over my shock of having a soldier just walk right up and join us whether he's invited or not, I catch up with them. I do wonder how soldiers can be so kind in one circumstance and so cruel in another.

When we reach our great building, Erik directs us to an open stairway rising outside a wide wall of ironwork that allows us to see into the first floor. I peer in, curious about what I see—cells with iron bars, and Japanese men in worn and wrinkled uniforms. The cells are arranged around an open space, like a courtyard. I do not like the idea of having Japanese soldiers nearby.

"I am sorry, but you must share this penitentiary with prisoners," Erik laughs. He must have sensed my curiosity. "Mostly, they are Japanese who must stay here until we decide what to do with them," he adds. "But they stay down here and you stay upstairs, except when you want to visit them."

"Visit them?" Tante Zus asks. My question, exactly. Why would anyone want to visit them?

"You will see," Erik answers with another smile, but this smile seems more like clenched teeth to me. He sets Edith on her feet. "Can you handle it from here, Ay-dith?" he asks. She nods her head and pulls herself up to the first step.

"Here, big sister can carry the luggage," he says, handing me the Edith-sized gunnysack. He extends his arm way out and dangles the bag by its drawstring. I think he understands. I like him, and he has the same name as my dead big brother.

I keep an eye on the first-floor prisoners until the long stairway takes me beyond the opening. The second floor is not divided into cells and, at first glance, seems to have no end in any direction. Only a few people here and there, but many cots lined up against the walls and out in the middle of the vast space. One wall is taken up with arched openings, filled in with iron bars. The openings let in air and light.

We find our space according to the numbers written on a piece of paper. It is up against one of the walls. We have five green canvas cots stretched over steel frames. No bedbugs, hurray! We take clean clothes out of our bags, stash the rest of our belongings under our cots, and set about finding a mandi bak. On the way down the stairs, my eyes are drawn, again, to the Japanese prisoners in their iron cells—cruel little cages, but so much better than they gave my mother.

We find something far better than a mandi bak—a building full of shower stalls. With doors on them. Ah, privacy! Another building holds mandi baks, and a third, toilets—everything in stalls. Thank you, thank you, thank you. We shower and Marijke and I help our aunt wash the filthy traveling clothes. Oh, it is so good to be clean again.

As soon as we are clean, we must find our way around our new home. I doubt if we will spend much time up in that huge room full of green cots.

We come to rest at one of the tables, and hurray, we learn it is time for dinner. We pick up our trays outside and follow the others into the kitchen. *Frikadel goreng!* I love meatballs. When the Indies lady puts the rice on my tray she says, "Is that enough?"

I think I am going to get along fine at Fort Willem II.

After dinner we make a visit to the toilets—real toilets—and then "home" to our cots. Before long, we hear strange cries and groaning, like people are being hurt. We also hear laughter, women's laughter. Whatever in the world? I want to go down the stairs to see what this is all about.

"No!" Tante Zus says firmly.

"But Tante, I will come right back," I argue.

"Ilse, you are never to go downstairs when you hear these sounds. Do you understand?"

I glare at my aunt, as I think she is being unreasonable. I nod, just the tiniest bit, as I'm not sure whether I will obey this order. She reads my mind, as usual.

"If you do, I will give you a beating that will make YOU cry. Now, do you understand?"

I understand that Tante Zus is very serious about this. She has never given me a beating, and I would like to keep it that way. I nod my head more enthusiastically.

The wailing and groaning stop, but in the morning my eyes fly open when I hear screaming. It is a man's voice, and he is in terrible pain. And then another joins him. Tante Zus and the others all wake up. We look around, and most of the other people are already out of their beds and gone. They must be early risers here. Or perhaps we are late risers. I see the sun is bright in the sky.

"Tante Zus, I'm hungry," says René. Exactly what I'm thinking, but I don't know if Tante Zus will allow us to go down the stairs while the screaming is going on. I am afraid breakfast will be over if we don't go soon.

We all pull on our clothes and put on our sandals, and finally Tante Zus gives in.

"Do not look," Tante commands, and as we go down the stairs, she gets between us and the big ironwork wall. Something horrible is happening in the court area, and now that we are outside, the screams and the shrieks of the men are much worse. We can hear women yelling, too, but not in pain, and some of them are laughing. I honestly don't want to look. Maybe there was a time when I would have been curious enough to sneak a peek, but I have seen enough horror and I do not want to see any more.

Once down the stairs and past the prison courtyard, we all take off fast for the kitchen. Marijke and I watch kids play while we wait in the line outside the gaar keuken. We have not missed breakfast, thank heaven.

We have all put on some weight, and Tante Zus no longer has skeleton cheeks. She is really very pretty, and I think that KNIL soldier, Erik, was flirting with her. But she is married. We are hoping her husband, Oom Ruud, is still alive. I wonder why Tante Zus has no children, but I have never asked. She is thirty-nine years old. Mam would be forty-two. I squeeze my eyes closed for a second. I wish you were here, Mam, I think for the hundred-thousandth time.

Marijke and I finish our very excellent porridge at the same time, and we take our trays to the big bin for washing. Then we head for the post office which, we hear, has pictures of Japanese soldiers. The authorities are trying to find the ones who should be punished for war crimes. The walls are filled with pictures and new ones go up every day, the lady behind the desk tells us. If we can find the one who beat Mam that night of her arrest, he might be put on trial to pay for his crime. Oh, yes, I would like to find that one.

"What do you think, Mieke?" I ask. I am using her nickname. She is becoming more like a friend, a very pretty eight-year-old, quite grown up for her age.

She points to two of the photos. "These look a little bit like him," she says, but I can tell she is not confident.

"Hmmm," I say. "A little bit, but I am not sure." We do not want the wrong person to be punished. Mam would be proud of her daughters' fair-mindedness. In spite of everything that has happened to us, we do not believe in *satu salah, semuah salah.*

"They all look so much alike," she sighs, and I agree with her.

We spend a few extra minutes checking the photos again, just in case we missed our man, but we find nothing. We go back outside to play. Marijke runs to join a gotrik game just starting. I want to find a game of bikkelen I can join. I look around to find some unsuspecting bikkelen players who do not yet know they will be doomed to lose.

On a regular basis, former prisoners were turned loose on their former captors at Fort Willem II. The pain they inflicted was fully as brutal as the pain they had suffered. They beat, they kicked, they even mutilated the Japanese prisoners. Tante Zus never participated, nor did she watch or allow me to watch. What stuck in my ears were the triumphant shrieks of the women as they performed the torture. I knew what my mother would have said about it. Torture is torture, no matter who is committing it, and it is always wrong.

Chapter 30.
Reunion

We were on a timer at Fort Willem II. We had only so long to find a place to go. Some of the refugees went to New Guinea, some to Australia, and some were able to "go home," war-torn as it was. If none of those things worked, the default plan was repatriation to the Netherlands. As citizens of the Dutch East Indies, we were citizens of the Netherlands.

I was ambivalent about that prospect. In the Netherlands we would be safe from pemudas and the Indonesian Republican Army, but the Emerald Girdle was my home and I could not imagine living anywhere else. Besides, to repatriate meant to be sent back to where we came from. True, we were Dutch citizens and proud of it, but how could we be repatriated to a place we had never lived? Where else could we go, however, without money, without protection? It was a dilemma and time was running out.

Always, the Red Cross people walk around with stacks of telegrams in their hands, calling names. "The family of Hans Brudjek." "Celeste Merkele." "Philomene Koetsel, mother of Poul Christje." It goes on and on, and although I do not actually listen, I always have an ear open for my own name, Evelijn Veere, or for my aunt's, Doyer.

In the middle of a game of bikkelen, I hear it: "Zus Doyer and the family of Hendrik Evelijn Veere." The Red Cross lady is twenty feet away, calling our names. In panic, I look for Tante Zus. I want her to receive the news, whatever it is. I am not sure I could read the telegram after all this time without schooling, and I am not willing to admit this to the lady in the Red Cross uniform.

I open my mouth and yell, "Tante Zus!"

Tante Zus appears with Edith on one hip and René jogging along beside her. Marijke comes running from her gotrik game. We all stand before the Red Cross worker who is, by this time, calling out someone else's name.

"Zus Doyer," my aunt says. She is breathless. "You just called my name. And these are the children of Hendrik Evelijn Veere."

"Oh, yes, my dear. I have a telegram for you. From someone very important, I see."

It must be a message from Pap—a very important person, she said. I feel a little prick of pride in being the daughter of an important person again.

Tante Zus puts Edith down and takes the message. I can see her hand is shaky.

"Bert!" my aunt shouts.

Oom Bert? The telegram is from my mother's older brother? But he and his family left for Australia when the Japanese moved into Java. How could we be hearing from Oom Bert?

"Oh, Ilse, your Oom Bert is back. He is living in Batavia and he has been looking for us for months."

In Batavia? He is safe in Batavia when the rest of us are staying in a penitentiary?

"His address says 'Commodore-General Bert Fiedeldij.' He must be back with the Netherlands East Indies Air Force."

An important man, Oom Bert. I suppose he was important before the war, too, with gold all over his uniform. But then he was just my uncle who flew his own airplane and brought us treats and gadgets.

"He will be here in two days! Two days, my darling schatjes!" Tante Zus grabs René and swings him around in a little dance. People are looking at us.

I am happy, but I am also puzzled. Why are we hearing from Oom Bert and not my father? Is he dead, or has he just forgotten about us? Why would such a thought come into my head? I am instantly sorry for it. And there is another worrisome thing. When Tante Zus reads Oom Bert's telegram word for word, it says he will come for Zus, Mies, and the children. We will have to tell him Mam is dead.

In spite of my concerns, I can hardly wait to see Oom Bert. Tante Zus tells us we are going to live in Oom Bert's big house on a military base in Batavia. Some people call it Jakarta now, but it is Batavia to me—the capital. Imagine! We will have to relearn a lot about polite manners, and we will surely have to use utensils for eating. All the time, not just for five minutes per meal. And I will have to resume my schooling, another worrisome issue. But my worries are far outshadowed by my joy. My uncle is coming to rescue us from Fort Willem II and from repatriation.

The minute I wake I remember this is the day Oom Bert is coming to get us. It is difficult to behave normally when we are about to move to Batavia. I want to giggle. We pack up our belongings and haul our gunnysack luggage to breakfast with us. We are ready to go.

At breakfast we sit where we can watch the entrance to the fort. Marijke and I get invited to play bikkelen, but I am so distracted by every bit of movement around the gate, I toss wild or miss my scoops. I will not be leaving this place undefeated, but it doesn't matter to me now.

I see Tante Zus and the little ones walking toward us. I realize they are not so little any more. René has turned seven, and now that he is eating well, he is a sturdy boy, light caramel skin, looking very much like Pap. Edith is a bright little two-and-a-half-year old with beautiful bronze skin, no longer shaky on her feet. Her eyes sparkle and dance, like Mam's. So do Marijke's.

"Come, children, shall we take a look at the latest pictures?" Tante asks.

The five of us stroll to the post office, never taking our eyes off the front gate. In the photo gallery we do not find our man, the Kempeitai soldier who abused our mother. This is our last chance, so we are a little disappointed, but that doesn't seem to matter, either.

Walking out of the post office, we see a very long, very sleek black car roll by—a limousine with a chauffeur, I think. The back window is rolled down. The man inside takes off his sunglasses and turns his head toward us.

"Bert!" my aunt screams, and she runs toward the car, leaving us behind. The car stops, Oom Bert jumps out, and they are hugging. Oom Bert has lifted his little sister right off her feet, and I can hear Tante Zus laughing and crying all at the same time.

I take Edith's hand, Marijke pushes René along, and we walk up to our aunt and uncle. Oom Bert hugs René and Marijke in a bundle, lifting them both off the ground. He turns to me, his arms out. I resort to my old trick and drop down to my knees beside Edith.

"This is Edith," I say. "She is two-and-a-half!" I love my Oom Bert, but he is a man, and he is wearing a uniform. I have to fight down my fear.

Edith cooperates with an adorable smile, and she gets the hug.

We wait in the limousine while Oom Bert and Tante Zus talk. I suppose Tante Zus is telling my uncle about Mam. Then they disappear into the Red Cross headquarters building, probably to check out of Fort Willem II.

Two brown leather seats face each other. I take in a deep breath and remember how the saddles smelled when the katjung cleaned them with special soap and then rubbed them until they gleamed. I am suddenly sad to think that René and Marijke hardly remember ever being in a car or on a horse, and Edith has nothing to remember.

When my aunt and uncle return, the driver starts the car, and we are off. Oom Bert leans across to René. "How would you like to go for a ride in an airplane, my boy?"

When we entered our uncle's home in Batavia at the beginning of 1946, we re-entered the life we had left in 1942. Oom Bert took us shopping for our first round of clothing and for our first real shoes in nearly four years. They were white and they fit our feet perfectly, with nothing hanging out the front. At the same time, he bought Tante Zus an electric sewing machine and she put her talent to work. I can see every detail of the beautiful white dress she fashioned for me, with little pink roses and lots of ruffles, a work of art.

We sat up to a real table, on real chairs, and had linen napkins to put in our laps. Of course we had to eat with forks and spoons and knives, but that was a small price to pay. Then, real beds—big beds with box springs and mattresses—with silky smooth sheets and fluffy pillows. It would be impossible to put into words how that felt to me when I was twelve, going on thirteen, and I had come to the end of a living nightmare.

Chapter 31.
Tjakranagara Way

In 1946 while the rest of the world nursed its war wounds, bombs were still falling on the Dutch East Indies, but we children were safe and secure in the heart of the Dutch East Indies military headquarters, unbothered by war or politics. Now that our lives had been set back on course, where was Pap? We would learn that next.

❦

Tante Zus is tutoring us. I am the only one who has ever been to school. René and Marijke are starting from scratch, but honestly, they seem to be progressing better than I am. It is just so hard to concentrate on letters and numbers when I would rather dance and draw. I am embarrassed that I have forgotten so much. Marijke is reading aloud to our aunt when we hear the doorbell chime. Tante Zus leaves us to answer the door, rather quickly I think. Maybe she would rather be dancing and drawing, too. We are a lot alike.

I look out the window and see a woman in a Red Cross uniform walking back to an official Red Cross car. This is very curious.

Tante Zus comes back into the dining room where we have been gathered around the table. I recognize the piece of paper she holds in her hand—a telegram, like the ones we used to see at Fort Willem.

"What is it? What is it?" Marijke and René ask. They remember the telegram that brought us such good news before. But I see the expression on our aunt's face, like she has been doused with ice-cold water. She sits back down, sort of easing herself into the chair. She is giving herself time to get control of her feelings, I can tell.

"My darlings, this is from your father—"

"From Pap?" "He is alive?" "Where is he?" We are all asking questions at the same time, except Edith who does not remember Pap. I'm not sure she even understands what a father is.

"Hush, now, and I will read the message."

It says that Pap is living in Bandung. He has just learned of Mies's death, and he wants his children to come home.

The others are all talking, but I am silent. Then I burst into tears. Tante Zus comes over to my chair and holds me tight against her. She is crying, too. The poor little ones just stare at us. They do not know what to think. I do not know what to think, either. Everything that has happened since I last saw Pap now churns around in my head, pushing hard to come out.

Yes, I want to see my father, to fall into his arms, to tell him how Mam died, to tell him about the blood and about her suffering. I want him to hold me and to cry with me, and to tell me how sorry he is that all these things happened, and to help me remember Mam in the good days, and to help me dissolve this solid block of ice that stays in the middle of my gut every single minute of every single day, my grief. I want to tell him about the hell-hut in the jungle where I waited to be burned alive or beheaded. I want him to tell me there is nothing, ever, to fear any more, and I want to believe him.

But I do not know if it will happen that way. I am afraid—more afraid than I have been since we carried Mam from her death cell. I am afraid that if I go back to my father I will lose Tante Zus. Please, God, do not let that happen. Please, please, please.

It is arranged. In two days Oom Bert will take us to Bandung in his airplane. My mind is numb with my fear of losing Tante Zus, but I don't voice my fear. I know it is childish, but I hope that if I don't talk about it the nightmare will go away. We pack our belongings in new leather suitcases. The last to go into my suitcase is my white dress with the pink rosebuds. It lies on top, on a bed of white tissue to protect it. Oh, it is so beautiful.

The last night in Oom Bert's house, Tante Zus comes into my room and sits on the edge of my bed.

"Ilse, I have something to tell you," she says. Her face is grim, her jaw set the way it is when she must face something unpleasant or dangerous.

I raise my head off the pillow and sit up straight. I sense that I do not want to be lying down when I hear what she has to say.

"You know how much I love you and the children."

Yes, I know that, so I nod, but I do not speak, as if by not speaking I can change what she is going to say.

"You know, too, how much I have always wanted a child of my own."

I thought we were now her children—Edith, René, Marijke, and me. But I remain silent.

"It might be different if I knew whether I would ever see Oom Ruud again, or if I had a home of my own."

What might be different? I lower my head, as if I am praying that she will stop now, kiss me goodnight, and leave. But I know she has more to say. Tante Zus hitches herself further up on the high bed so she is closer to me.

"I have found a little girl, a very sickly little girl who will need a lot of care. No one wants to give her a home."

So? I raise my eyes but not my head. The only light in the room comes from the outside courtyard, but I can see her eyes glistening and I know tears are about to spill over. My eyes are dry.

"Ilse, I am going to adopt this little girl—Irene is her name—and the two of us are going to live in Holland."

It starts deep in my gut and pushes out through my throat, and I hear myself screaming, "Noooooooooo!"

Tante Zus starts to put her arms around me, but I push against her soft body to launch myself backward against the wooden headboard. I feel the carved figures digging into my back.

"You can't leave us," I shout. "WE are your children—not that other girl." I choke on my words. My throat, so open a second ago, is now blocked by tears and sobbing.

"Ilse, you are your father's children, and he wants you back."

"I don't care," I cry through snot and tears. "I want you." Then it comes out, what I really want. "I want my mami."

Tante Zus is sobbing, too, and when she holds out her arms this time, I fall into them.

We cling to each other and rock side to side on this great pillow-soft bed until I am calm enough to say what is in my mind. I sit back and wipe my face and nose on the silken sheet.

"Tante Zus, you want children? We will be your children. We will be very good, I promise. I will make sure of it. The others do as I say."

"Of course, my precious angel. But you cannot be my children while your father wants you back. It is the law."

"Who cares about the law?" I spit. "What did the law do for my mother when they put her into a little box?"

"It is different now, Ilse. We have to abide by the Dutch law."

"You promised her, Tante Zus. You promised you would never leave us. How can you go back on your promise?"

"He is your father."

The argument goes on and on, but it all comes down to, "Ilse, he is your father. If he wants you back, there is nothing I can do. It is the law."

It becomes clear to me that I am powerless to change it, so I struggle to accept it. I decide I will work hard to be a good daughter and a good big sister. It will be a labor of love, something I can for Mam—I will do everything I can to stand in for her in this family. But the best reason for going back: I will be able to tell Pap about everything that has happened to us, and then he and I will help each other and the younger ones to deal with the grief and the nightmares. Oh yes, Pap and I have so much to tell each other, but mostly I have to tell him about Mam.

Marijke and René and Edith are excited about the plane ride, and they are excited about seeing their papi. I try not to let my glum mood ruin their happiness. I hope their happiness will seep into my glum mood.

We fly low, approaching the airport at Bandung. I am beginning to feel a sense of homecoming.

"See, Mieke, there is the Cikapundung River where we used to swim."

"You, Ilse, not me. It was forbidden because it had poop floating in it."

Everyone laughs, including me. I can see that Tante Zus is glad for the little joke.

Oom Bert lands the plane and pulls it up to a low building. A black limousine is waiting for us on the other side of the building. The driver and Oom Bert pile the luggage into the trunk. No gunnysacks, this time.

Oom Bert opens the door for Tante Zus, and she climbs in. Then he swings Edith up into the car.

"Goodbye, little one," he says.

"Goodbye!" I say in surprise. "Aren't you coming with us, Oom?"

"No, Ilse, I am a busy man," he answers with a smile, but his eyes aren't smiling. Something seems wrong here. He gives me a hug, and then hugs René and Marijke. Edith gives him a great smooching kiss, and I think he is holding back tears.

He says to the driver, "Tjakranagara Way. Here is the number." Then, to Tante Zus, "See you in a little while. Good luck." He closes the door, and we wave to him through the open window.

See you in a little while? Tante Zus is not going to stay with us until we get used to our new home? Oom Bert cannot even ride along with us? And why does she need luck? Do they know something they are not telling us? I realize I am holding my breath again, as I do when I am nervous.

I hardly notice the city even though we pass by places I would recognize. After all, this is my birthplace! The others chatter with Tante Zus, and I hear, "Oh, look at this," and "Oh, look at that." We enter a tree-lined boulevard and in a few blocks, I see "Tjakranagara Weg" on a street sign. We turn right and then make another right into a driveway lined with hibiscus on one side. We park in front of the pavilion, a little cottage in front of the main house. I wonder if this is where our father will greet us. It is customary to entertain guests in the pavilion. A pretty woman waves to us from the window of the pavilion. We wave back. But no Pap. I guess we are not guests, technically.

The driver opens the doors for us. We all get out and stand by the car, then Tante Zus takes Edith's hand and walks toward the main house. We walk across the spacious verandah. Tante Zus lifts the brass knocker, lets it fall, and stands aside. When the door opens, my father is standing there, and then we are all laughing and crying. Well, Tante Zus is doing neither, and Edith is hanging back.

"Pap," I say over and over when it is my turn for a hug.

Tante Zus pulls my father aside, and they talk. I can hear the hum of their voices, but not what they say. Pap snaps his fingers to summon the driver to bring the luggage. Then my father says, "Come in," and I walk toward the door.

"No, no, not you," he says, and I realize it is Tante Zus who has been invited in. I am embarrassed. "You children, go play," he says, and I wonder what we are supposed to play with.

The door closes behind my father and Tante Zus as the first suitcase arrives. The driver sets it next to the door and goes back for another. With nothing else to do, we sit at one of the tables on the verandah. Edith climbs into my lap and Marijke and René chatter about the yard and the garden and whether they should go exploring. Before they have a chance, however, the lady from the pavilion appears.

She is tall and slender, and although her hair is dark, her skin is quite fair. Definitely Indiesa, but leaning toward European looks. Another slender lady is walking behind her, carrying a tray full of treats. Lemonade, it looks like, and cookies.

"Good morning! My name is Noes, but you will be calling me something else," says the first lady, and her eyes twinkle in a friendly manner. "And I already know your names!" She points to each of us and says our names. I smile, but I don't say anything, and the others act shy.

"This is my sister," she says as the other lady sets the tray on the table. They hand out the goodies, which are delicious. The lady and her sister want to know how old each of us is, how we liked the airplane ride, what we like to eat, and how we like school. The children are on their best behavior, but they don't know how to answer the last one.

"We haven't been to school," I say.

The women look shocked, so I decide I should explain more.

"Not unless you count the nuns' place at Camp Halmaheira."

They both look puzzled.

"Of course I went to school before we moved to De Hotel, but that was a long time ago."

Ah, they seem to understand now, so I feel more comfortable.

"But I have forgotten almost everything I learned there."

Their eyes blink and open wide, and I think I may have said too much.

"Of course," says the lady whose name is Noes. "We have all been through difficult times." Then she changes the subject. "Would you like to play in the garden?"

René and Marijke jump down from their chairs and scamper out onto the lawn. I follow them in order to keep an eye on Edith. The ladies watch us for a few minutes, and then they disappear, with the empty tray, back into the pavilion.

The house and the gardens are very much like I remember from our life before—the main house, with flowers in front and vegetable gardens in back, and servants' houses against the brandgang wall in the back. I don't see any signs of servants, though. We wander around for awhile, and then Marijke says she would like to make hibiscus dolls.

"I think we should ask permission to pick the flowers," I tell her, and she scoots off to the pavilion to see if it's okay.

"Yes, my dear," I hear the lady say. "You may pick as many as you want."

We heap the blossoms on the verandah table. The Noes lady—I don't know what I am supposed to call her, as she did not give us her last name— sits with us for a few minutes and tells us how pretty our dolls are. We find out the other lady lives in the pavilion. I wonder where Noes lives, if not with her sister. When the lady goes back to the pavilion Marijke runs after her to give her a doll—a nice yellow one with a big skirt. I can see the lady is pleased.

We make more dolls—I help Edith—and finally René gets bored and goes to turn somersaults and cartwheels on the thick grass, even though he has on his good clothes. I don't tell him to stop. I am tired of waiting, and I would like to go inside the house to see what is taking so long. Maybe Tante Zus is talking my father into changing his mind. I am glad my father is alive. I am glad, I guess, that he wants us to be with him. But I would be so much happier if we could continue to live with Oom Bert in Batavia and just visit my father from time to time in Bandung.

Finally the big door opens. My father leans against the doorframe as Tante Zus walks toward us. She has been crying,

I can tell. I hold my breath, hoping she will take us back to the limousine that waits at the pavilion. She picks up Edith first.

"Goodbye, my darling schatje," she says.

My breath flies out of my lungs and leaves my heart flat, thud, in the pit of my stomach, and something spills out of my insides that makes me want to howl, or to run, or to smash something. One by one, she hugs each of us and tells us how much she loves us. By the time she gets to me, her tears are streaming. Edith is too little to understand, but I can see that Marijke and René are confused. They do not know about the sickly little girl, or about Tante Zus moving to the Netherlands. I suppose I will have to explain it to them.

She hugs me hard, and I try to hug back just as hard, but I think she can tell I am angry. My anger has dried up my tears for the moment, but I know I will cry plenty later. Then she looks at each of us one more time, turns, and walks toward the waiting limousine. It turns around in the driveway. One last wave, and she is gone. My father waits until the car turns onto Tjakranagara Way, and then he calls to us.

"Come in, come in," he says, and we pass by the suitcases on our way to an elegant parlor. He invites us to sit down, so we choose our chairs and I hold Edith. Pap takes a seat in a big rattan rocker with flowers printed on the cushion. It reminds me of Mam's chair in the old days, but of course the Japanese took our furniture when they took our house, so nothing is the same.

"You look well," he says to all of us, in general. "Much bigger than the last time I saw you," he chuckles. He does not say anything about Mam's not being here, but I guess he doesn't want to make us feel sad right now. He asks us how we have been and whether we have been studying. We answer politely, except for Edith who only stares at him and presses hard against me.

So, I wonder, when do we get to start talking about what has happened since De Hotel and the day he disappeared down the hall, just ahead of bayonets? When do we tell him about Halmaheira and the torture and the hunger and the snail soup and the dysentery and the squatting holes and the escape to Tante Annie's and the goat and the pemuda jail and the Gurkhas and the airplanes shooting at us? Mostly, when do I get to tell him about Mam in the blistering hot cell and about Mam's bleeding to death as I held her?

"Well," Pap clears his throat. "Much has happened since we were together last, eh? But we don't want to live in the unpleasant past. It is over and done with, eh? We must now look to the future, and I have something to tell you. An announcement!" He leans forward in his chair and smiles to let us know we will be pleased.

We all lean toward him, waiting to hear what our father has to announce.

"You are going to have sisters and brothers—two of each. They are your ages, so you will be great friends."

He waits for our reaction, but we don't have any because this doesn't make any sense. How can we have more brothers and sisters? We haven't seen Pap for years and Mam is dead.

"They are Noes's children—the lady you have been visiting with on the verandah. Her real name is Rosalie Josephine Brueur."

As if that explains anything, but at least I can call her Mrs. Brueur now.

"We are going to be married, you see." Pap is still smiling, like he is giving us a gift. "You are to have a new mother!"

A new mother? The lady from the pavilion? I struggle to understand what I am hearing.

My father sits back in his chair to finish his announcement. "Her children have been calling me 'Pap,' so now I want all of you to call her 'Mam.'"

I know Pap is waiting for me to say something, but I cannot say what is in my heart and on my tongue. *How could you,* I am thinking. *How could you bring another woman in to replace my mother? How could you ask us to accept new brothers and sisters who apparently had the comfort of your parenting while we walked barefoot and hid in forests? Was my mother dead yet, when these new brothers and sisters started calling you "Pap"?*

Thus began my long silence, and thus began our new life as a blended family under my father's roof.

Chapter 32.
The White Dress

My stomach still tightens when I think of that first day in the house on Tjakranagara Way. It set the tone for family relationships over the next four years in Bandung and for many years beyond that.

For one thing, I knew that I would never call Rosalie Josephine Brueur "Mam." I had only one Mam; she died in my arms at Camp Halmaheira. From that first day until the day my stepmother died, I never called her anything. If I needed to speak with her, I waited until she looked at me and then I started talking. If she didn't look at me, I simply said "Excuse me" and told her what I needed to say. As a last resort, I tapped her lightly on the shoulder to get her attention. It became a point of contention that grew as time went on, a battle line drawn between a stubborn girl who could have made her own life easier and a stubborn woman who should have understood but didn't.

The other battle line drawn that day was between "his children" and "her children." I think, now, that my father was trying to play fair, to treat all eight of us equally. But in doing so, he fell into a common trap for stepparents—he overcompensated on the side of the stepchildren.

Here they come, into the parlor, the woman in the pavilion and her children who now call my father "Pap." Where have these children been, our new brothers and sisters? In their rooms, I guess, while we played by ourselves and had lemonade outside. Well, they are here now, and I have to admit to being curious about them. I have been the oldest my whole life, ever since my brother died when I was a baby. Now, suddenly, I have a big sister.

"Ditte, here, is fourteen—one year older than you, Ilse. So you will not be the boss any more, heh, heh. Isn't that right, Ditte?" my father jokes. Ditte smiles at me. She does not seem like a bossy person. She is just a little taller than I am, dark brown hair, slender like her mother, with big brown eyes that crinkle when she smiles.

Pap reaches out to a boy with a mop of very straight dark brown hair. He comes up to Pap's nose. "This is Fred. He is eleven, but very grown up for his age. He will be a great help to you all, eh, Fred?" My father puts his arm around Fred's shoulders and gives him a quick squeeze, like men do. I can see that Fred is pleased. With himself, I think.

"You bet, Pap!"

Hearing this stranger call my father "Pap" jolts me and I catch my breath. I nod in the direction of Fred and do my best to smile.

Next, I meet Bolle whose real name is Irma. She is my age—only three weeks younger—and I can't figure out why they call her Bolle which means round, like a ball. She is exactly my height and very pretty, with a dimple in her chin and long, dark brown hair, very shiny. She has breasts and a narrow waist. She is slender, not round in the least.

Marijke and René look like they can hardly wait to go play with Robby who is eight years old, right in between René who is seven and Marijke who is nine. Robby is a sturdy little fellow, with brown hair that has been cut under a bowl, I think. Marijke will have the little boys playing Gotrik in no time.

Three-year-old Edith is still the baby.

"Ah, little Edith, you are the only one without a brother or a sister near your age," says Pap, once the introductions are over.

Marijke and René have already run off with Robby, so they do not hear our father's next piece of news.

"But we will rectify that soon." He grins, wide, and his eyes warm up. He pats the woman's belly. "In about six months, you shall have a new baby sister or brother to play with."

"Oh, Jong," she says, looking very happy, but a little embarrassed.

I look around to see who else is in the room, someone named Jong. But then I realize she is talking to my father. The name means "boy" and I wonder why she calls him that. As for the new baby, I am glad I won't have to worry about this one starving to death. The woman still looks flat in the belly. Well, maybe a little bulge in the front of her flared cotton skirt, but not so you would notice right away. She has a very nice figure.

I wonder if they are married already.

"I guess you all want to visit and get to be good friends, eh?" my father says. It is the very thing I want least to do right now. "After all, you are brothers and sisters!" He picks up Edith and they leave the room.

The cook saves us—Ditte, Bolle, Fred and me—from being left alone in the parlor to become good friends. She comes in to announce the midday meal. She does not look like my babu kokki, but she smiles right at me and I sense I will be welcome in her kitchen.

Thank heaven Marijke, René, and I have gotten used to the fork and knife, so we do not disgrace ourselves at the table. Pap considers good manners important, I remember. I help Edith whose three-year-old manners can be forgiven, and it gives me something to do so I don't have to chatter on and on like Marijke and my brother are doing.

After the meal, my father tells us our plans for the afternoon.

"We need to introduce you to your new home. After that, we can all take a little rest, and then you can get to work putting your things away in your new rooms."

Pap and the woman—I suppose I can call her my "step" mother—take us around the house. From the dining room we go out the door to the wide concrete *gang,* the open roofed-over hallway that leads to the kitchen and mandi bak. The mandi bak, shower, and water closet are at the end of the long gang.

Edith tugs on my hand, and I take her into the water closet. She is a big girl now, and I hold the *botol* to direct the stream of cleansing water as she performs the *cebok,* cleaning herself very nicely. The squatting holes still come back to me at times. This is one of them, and I am grateful for a real water closet, with a real toilet and privacy. It is sparkling clean, but the stench of the squatting holes wafts over my memory.

"That's a good girl, Edith," I tell her. "Hurry, now."

I get a quick peek of the kitchen. I like it. It smells good, like my babu kokki's kitchen.

The stepmother opens the door to the storage room next to the kitchen—the *gudang.* "As you can see, we have not quite finished our plans for the gudang," she says. The room is full of boxes and loose items—toys, kitchen items, bicycles. "We plan to turn it into a bedroom for the younger boys. It won't be as pretty as the other bedrooms, but I doubt if you boys will mind that." She smiles at Robby and René who don't look particularly interested. I am sure they would rather be playing.

But I am very interested. A room right next to the kitchen. A place where I could be by myself and that I could keep neat and tidy, the way I like it, with no one getting into my belongings.

"Could I please have this room?" I ask.

Pap and the stepmother look puzzled, as if they didn't hear me correctly. Perhaps I didn't speak loudly enough.

"I would like very much to sleep in the gudang. May I have it, please?"

"But we thought you would like to share Bolle's lovely room," says the stepmother.

I glance at Bolle. I hope her feelings are not hurt.

"That would be very nice, too," I answer. "But I would like a room to myself, if that would be possible, and the gudang would be just fine. I do not mind being outside."

Pap frowns and looks at the stepmother. "Well," he says, "I suppose that would be all right, for now. We will be moving soon, so this is temporary, anyway."

Moving soon? Another surprise?

"Just to a larger house here in Bandung—on Gelria Straat," he adds, and I feel I have made a connection with my father. He sensed my unspoken question.

The room arrangements are settled. I will share Bolle's room until the gudang is ready. We all go to our rooms for the mid-dag dutje. I feel comfortable with Bolle—she is a nice girl—but I still look forward to closing the door behind me in my own room.

We take off our shoes and lie down on top of the bed in our clothes. Usually I would take off my outer clothes, but I feel awkward being in my underwear in front of a stranger. I guess she feels the same way. She turns toward one wall and I turn toward the other. We do not visit.

I rest, but I do not sleep. I gaze around Bolle's room. About the same size, I think, as my room in our house here in Bandung before the war. I see she has two small wardrobe closets, facing each other on opposite walls. I think of the great wardrobe closet Pap built for me, with the doll house in the middle. I know he loved me. He still does, I am sure.

When the bad memories come into my mind, or when I think of Tante Zus leaving, I stuff such thoughts down someplace where they won't hurt so much, and I think of Mam and Pap—before the war, when we lived in real houses like this one. But that hurts, too, just not as much. Finally Bolle stirs and sits up.

"You have a pretty room," I say.

"Thank you, Ilse." She sits up and stretches. "Would you like to start unpacking? I can help you."

"That would be nice. But what about the gudang? Should I wait until it is ready?"

"Oh, that could be days," she says. "My mother has given us an extra wardrobe, for your clothes. Don't you want to free them from the suitcase?"

Am I being suspicious to think she is just curious about what I have in my suitcase? No matter. I would like to hang up my dresses. They are wrinkled enough by now—no sense pressing the wrinkles in deeper.

The huge bag stands against the wall, outside the door. I wonder who put it there. I didn't see a djongos in the house, so it must have been Pap. Except for the kokki, I guess we have no servants here. Where would they come from? The désas? I shudder and lug the suitcase through the door and across the smooth tile floor. Bolle helps me heave it up onto the bed.

"Whew, it's heavy!" she says, and I agree. It might be nice to have a sister my age, to share the burdens.

"Were you ever in a camp?" I ask, in a sudden rush of curiosity.

"A camp?"

"A concentration camp—you know, with the Japanese?"

Bolle frowns and shakes her head. "No, we never had to go to a concentration camp," she answers. "Why?"

"Just wondered."

She doesn't ask if I was ever in a camp. I'm not sure that I would want to talk about it, but I won't talk about anything unless she asks.

I pop the heavy metal clasps and lay open the lid of the suitcase. On the top is the white dress. Bolle sucks in her breath through her open mouth like you do when you have a great surprise.

"Oh, look—how beautiful," she says. "And there are more!" She can see another dress, folded up under the tissue, and glimpses of more under that. She runs to the door and throws it open.

"Ditte, Ditte, come and look at Ilse's beautiful dresses!"

In an instant, we have not only Ditte, but Fred and Pap and the stepmother in the room. I have laid the white dress out on the bed, and one by one, I lay out the others. I admit, I am proud of my dresses, some store bought, but most from the clever needle of Tante Zus. It is fun to show them off, and the others say, "Ooh!" and "Ah!" as I bring them out. There are five, altogether. Fred peers into the bag—I think he is interested in what other treasures I might have tucked away in there. I'm going to have to watch out for him.

The stepmother comes in for a closer look, and Ditte runs her hand over the dresses, one by one. I can see she loves them. Even Pap has a big smile on his face. I think he is proud that his daughter is so well dressed. I feel happy about that.

"Ah, so many dresses!" he says. "And each a work of art!"

I nod in agreement.

"More than you and Ditte have, eh, Bolle?" he says.

They both nod their heads. "Many more!" says Bolle.

"I have only one good dress!" says Ditte.

"Then you must share with your sisters, Ilse," Pap says. "You are all about the same size."

What? I hold my breath.

"Go on Ditte, Bolle—select a dress. Ilse has so many, she will be happy to give one to each of you."

Surely everyone in the room can see that is not true. Ditte and Bolle hesitate.

"Go on, go on," Pap says, and he makes a shooing motion with his hand. "Take what you like."

Ditte and Bolle both grab for the white dress with the pink rosebuds, but Ditte gets it first. Bolle takes another one, but that doesn't matter. It is the white dress I want back.

"Oh, Pap, please, not the white dress—"

"Hush, Ilse, you have plenty of dresses left."

"But Tante Zus made the white dress especially for me." I stammer, I am so desperate for him to understand. But instead of understanding, his smile disappears and his face turns hard.

"Nonsense, Ilse. You must learn to share."

I watch as Ditte carries my beautiful white dress out the door. She is almost dancing. My heart tightens down in my chest, and I burst into tears.

"That will be enough, Ilse. You are part of a family now. The sooner you understand that and learn to share, the better." Pap leaves the room, the stepmother and Fred behind him. Bolle hangs up her new dress and tiptoes out to leave me alone with my tears.

Chapter 33.
Battle Scenes

When we moved back to Bandung, I did not have an elementary school education. While my step-siblings had been studying at home during the Japanese occupation and the Bersiap Period, I had been stealing food and avoiding pemudas. Marijke and René were the right age for elementary school, so they fit in. But a girl like me, thirteen years old and already a young woman, could not sit in a classroom with little children. So Pap—the elementary school principal—decided to teach me at home until my skills improved enough to pass the *Toelatings Exam* that would allow me to enter the *Hogere Burger School,* the academic high school my father chose for me.

Pap's office at home became my classroom. A pleasant place, Pap's office in the house on Gelria Straat—flooded with light from tall windows, furnished with an immense mahogany desk, always polished to a high gloss, and a square mahogany study table with cushioned chairs. A rattan couch with plump sage green cushions gave it a homey touch, a place to meet with colleagues or the private students Pap tutored in advanced math and science. With his private students he was unfailingly patient. Not so with his own daughter, however.

With a full-fledged revolution going on, war must have been seething all around us, but my attention was occupied by the war seething within our own household. Most of the battle scenes took place in Pap's office. Our sessions together were torture for me. I have no idea what they were for him. He never apologized for his behavior.

"Are you stupid?" he shouts at me. "No, you are not stupid, so why is it taking you so long?"

I see his right hand twitching. I know what is coming next, and I try to finish the problem, but I realize the answer is not coming out right.

"Let me do it again, Pap—I see what I did wrong. Please!" I do not want a slap on the head.

He sits back in his chair around the corner of the study table. Our knees form a right angle. He closes his eyes, and his lips disappear into a straight-across line. I am being given more time. I hurry, and this time the answer falls into place. Oh, mathematics can be so difficult for me, but for once I have succeeded.

Pap looks over my paper. The numerals are very straight, the way he insists, and he is pleased. Thank heaven, I have avoided the slap.

"One more problem," he says, "to make sure it is not a fluke that you have done this correctly. Not from the book this time. I shall write one out."

My heart sinks. The problems he makes up are so much more difficult. He puts tricks into them, and I must be just as tricky to find them.

This time I find the trick in the percentage—it is a decimal, and I work out the problem very quickly.

Pap gifts me with a smile. "You are coming along, Ilse. It won't be long before you will be ready for the Toelatings Exam."

It can't come too soon because I can't take much more of his home schooling. Today is a good day, but tomorrow I may get a slap that will turn my head around. The uncertainty is the agony—I never know which it will be.

I must be in his good favor today because he assigns only three pages of math problems for practice, and only the even numbered problems. Hurray! It would be a good time to bring up the subject I have been dreading.

"Pap, I would like to talk to you about something that has been happening."

He looks at his wristwatch. "Hurry up about it."

"Someone has been getting into my wardrobe."

"Not that again, Ilse. I told you to take it up with Bolle."

"No, Pap, it is not Bolle. She would never mess up my things." Since our move to Gelria Straat, Bolle and I have shared a room. She is a very good roommate.

"Well, then, who?" He is getting impatient; his fingers drum on the edge of the study table.

"I think it is Fred."

Pap throws both hands up, over his head and fans them out. "Absurd!" The hands shake—one staccato movement, to punctuate his words. "Why would Fred come into your room? And what, of yours, could he possibly want?"

"I don't know, Pap, but everything in my top drawer was turned out on the floor, and the drawer was upside down beside my clothes. The last time this happened, it was my desk drawer, and my colored pencils were missing. Remember?"

"That is what YOU say, Ilse. I have no proof that such a thing happened."

"What kind of proof do you need, Pap? My colored pencils were in my desk, and now they're gone." My frustration is coming out in a high-pitched whine, which I hate. Why won't he take my word for it?

"I don't have time for this nonsense, Ilse. I have to go to my Association meeting." Pop stands up and tosses his teacher's manual—with the answers—into his desk and locks it. Too bad I don't have locks on my desk drawers. "Take it up with your mother. Or talk with Fred. In any case, don't bother me with it again."

Pop picks up his Netherlands Indies Education Association notebook—he is the treasurer—and leaves me seated at the table. I calm myself. I have an hour before the midday meal, when the rest of the family will be home from school. Perhaps I can talk with my stepmother about Fred. I find her in the kitchen, feeding baby Caddy in his high chair. I smell something spicy, and I see dozens of round *bitter bollen* lined up on the butcher-block table, ready to be popped into hot oil later. I love the little croquettes.

"This smells delicious," I say in the direction of my stepmother. I want to be friendly in the hope she will listen to me about Fred.

"Thank you, Miss Ilse," says the babu kokki and she bows slightly from the waist, in the old way.

Unfortunately, I still have to figure out a way to capture my stepmother's attention. I stand beside her and give Caddy a huge open-mouthed smile. That usually makes him laugh, but he's too busy taking in spoonfuls of sweet rice pudding. My stepmother does not acknowledge me. It would be so easy for her to look at me and say, "Ilse, did you have a good study session this morning?" and then we could have a cordial conversation. But she doesn't. She has two faces—the one she shows in front of my father, sweet and considerate toward his children, and the one she shows when he is not around, harsh and spiteful.

I sigh, more loudly than I meant to, and say, "Excuse me."

"Do you want something?" she says without looking up. Her voice is flat.

"Yes. Pap says I should talk to you about what is going on in my room when I am not there."

"And just what is going on?" she asks. Her eyebrows are high and the question is not friendly.

"Someone pulled out one of my wardrobe drawers and dumped everything on the floor. Then he left the drawer on the floor, upside down."

"He?" she says, and the eyebrows go even higher. "Do you think it is your brother?"

I know she means René, even though she and Pap preach to us all the time about how we are ALL brothers and sisters. I think Pap means it, but I can tell she doesn't.

"No, my brother wouldn't do anything like that." I take in a deep breath and hold it for a moment. Then I let it out with my words. "I think it is Fred."

She slams the baby spoon down on the high chair tray. Caddy jumps. She looks straight at me, and her eyes burn a hole right through me.

"Just who do you think you are?" she says, spitting out the words. "What makes you think Fred would want to come any-where near your wardrobe?"

"I have seen him coming out of my room. I know he goes in there." I am scared, but I am angry, too, and my eyes lock on hers.

"Remember, that is Bolle's room. He has a right to visit his own sister. If you don't want anyone going through your belongings, I suggest you keep them put away."

"They WERE put away—" I begin to protest.

"Don't bother me any more," she barks. "And leave my Freddy alone."

I leave the kitchen and return to my father's study. Perhaps I can finish my math problems before the afternoon study session.

When Pap and I meet in the den after the mid-dag dutje, I know she has talked to him and it is not going to be a good session.

"Why must you persecute your mother, Ilse? After all that woman has done for you, you cannot treat her with respect?"

I say nothing. What has she done for me besides give me grief?

"Well?" he shouts into my face.

"I treat her with respect," I say, but the words do not come out very convincingly.

"What?" he shouts even louder. I am sure the rest of the household is listening to this.

"I do treat her with respect, Pap. She does not treat me with respect."

Whack, across the side of my head. I didn't get my hand up in time.

"You lie! She works day and night for you children, and you—YOU, Ilse will not even call her Mam."

I stand still, straight, and tears spill out.

"Do you have any idea how much that hurts her?" he yells.

I know how much she SAYS it hurts her because I hear this from my father at least once a week. I do not believe for one minute it really hurts her because if she had such a tender heart, she would know how much it hurts me to be asked to deny my own mother. I cannot, will not call another woman "Mam." But I can't say these things because it only makes it worse.

"Can't you do this to make MY life easier?" he says for the millionth time. His voice is quiet now. "Can't you just open your mouth and call her 'Mam'?"

Oh, how I wish I could, but I can't. Maybe if you would respect my mother enough to let me talk about her, but you won't. I think this, but I do not say it any more because it is futile. He will just flare up again and tell me I have to forget the unpleasant past. Forget my mother? I am shaking with my silent sobs. He plants his feet wide apart and puts his fists on his hips. I cannot look at him, but I know he is staring at me. I think this battle is over, but no one won.

I am the only one at home during the day—the others are at school. And even after school hours, I am in the office working with Pap or studying by myself. The only other person allowed into Pap's den—my prison—is Fred because he does business for Pap. He takes his bicycle out every month and collects dues from the members of the Netherlands-Indies Education Association. When he brings the money in, he fills out the ledger page, who has paid and who has not, and then he puts the money in a blue pouch and locks it in the desk drawer that Pap uses for a safe. I do not look forward to those days when Fred sits at Pap's desk and acts like a big shot, but at least I am not alone.

Nor am I alone when Pap comes in to check my work and scream at me. "Wake up!" "Stop day dreaming!" "You cannot be so stupid!"

I am at the mahogany table after the mid-dag dutje, as usual, when Pap comes into the office.

"I am going to the bank to deposit the Association funds," he says. "I will check your work when I get back. Do you have any questions about it?"

I shake my head. The work today is easier than usual. He goes to the desk and unlocks the safe drawer. "What is this?" he says, more to himself than to me.

"Ilse, the money pouch is empty. Do you know anything about this?"

"No, Pap," I answer.

"Has Fred been here?"

"I haven't seen him today. He came in last night after he came home from collecting."

Pap looks puzzled, and he calls for Fred. This is a welcome distraction for me, so I listen.

"Where is the money you collected yesterday?" Pap asks.

"Right there in the pouch," Fred answers.

"No, it is not." Pap looks very stern, indeed. It is nice to see that look directed at someone besides me for a change.

"Well, that's where I put it. If it isn't there, I don't know where it is." Fred does not look very concerned. "Ilse saw me put it away," he adds. "She was here last night."

Pap turns to me. I am caught listening in.

"Yes, he had money on the desk last night. I didn't see him put it away."

"You lie!" The force of Fred's accusation makes me blink. "You saw me put it in the pouch and lock the pouch in the safe."

"Well, you probably did. I wasn't paying much attention." I do not know why Fred has gotten so angry, but I am automatically suspicious of him. "And I do not lie," I add just in case anyone cares.

Fred and I watch while Pap rummages around the desk. He probably hopes the money fell out of the pouch, or that Fred was forgetful and left it out.

Pap questions us both again, and then asks us to leave. Gladly! I am happy to have an afternoon off. Pap calls for my stepmother—a demanding call, not very civil. We cross paths in the dining room as she is hurrying to the office, and I am hurrying away from it.

Not long afterward, my stepmother appears at my bedroom door. "Your father wants to see you in the office," she says. I think her tone of voice is more congenial than usual, but when I look at her I see smugness. I don't know why she is smug, but I do know my hopes of a free afternoon are dashed; he will want me to study some more.

Pap slams the office door shut. His face is red and his eyes are filled with hate. I am stunned.

"Where is the money, Ilse?"

Why is he asking me? I do not deal with the money.

"I want the money back. Right now."

"Pap, I don't know where the money is. Why don't you ask Fred?"

He slaps me so hard, I bump into the desk chair and it tips over with a crash. I am still standing.

"You are in this room all day by yourself. Your mother tells me she hears you snooping around, opening drawers and cupboards."

"She lies, Pap. I never—" Another slap. My cheek stings.

"Do you want a beating? You will have a beating if you do not tell me the truth." He unbuckles his belt, and I watch as it slides out of the loops on his trousers.

"Please, Pap!" I am crying now, and afraid. "I am telling the truth. I don't have any idea where the money is." I back away from him, to put distance between that belt and me.

"You are the only one home during the day, and the only one who is allowed to come into this office," he says through clenched teeth. He steps toward me as he folds the leather belt in half. It looks like a billy club.

"What about Fred?" I cry. "He comes into—" The double leather strap across the side of my head catches me off guard, and I fall into the rattan couch and curl up into a ball, face down. I throw my arms over my head.

"I will not have a daughter who is a thief, and a liar too," he shouts, and the first blow lands across my back. "Are you ready to tell the truth?"

"I am telling the truth," I scream into the couch cushion.

The next blow lands, and the next, and the next. I think of Mam, as the blows rained upon her. Now I am in hell, too, for something I have not done, and all I can do is wail in terror.

The beating stops. "I am giving you one more chance to tell me the truth. Where is the money?"

His voice is quiet, so I lift my head to look at him. He looks exhausted. His shirttail has crept out of his trousers, and his red face has turned to the color of grey. Sweat is pouring down his forehead. I can tell he is finished with me, so I sit up.

"I don't have your money." My voice comes out in a quiet whimper. "Why can't you believe your own daughter?"

He leaves the room without answering.

❦

Sixty years later my daughter sat beside me at the table, trying to teach me the intricacies of email on my new, first-time-ever computer. I did not catch on very fast, and she became understandably impatient.

"Come on, Mom, it isn't that hard!" Her voice was harsh. She shifted in her chair and threw her hands up in the air, a quick movement.

My hand flew to the side of my head, and I burst into tears. My poor daughter, so compassionate, was bewildered.

"Mom, what's the matter?" she asked as she put her arm around me.

"You were just like my father," I said. And then we both cried.

Chapter 34.
Vindication

Two revolutions came to a head at the same time in 1950: the one in my homeland and the one in my home. While Indonesian nationalist leaders struggled to unite the myriad cultures of over 6,000 inhabited islands into one republic, Pap struggled to unite the twelve people under his roof—by now Caddy had a little sister, Judy—into one family.

Both were monumental tasks. One worked and one did not.

At last, I will attend the *Hogere Burger School*, the HBS, and be rid of Pap's home schooling, but I must pass the Toelatings Exam. I am ready, seated at one of the long tables in the HBS assembly hall, eager to take the test. I am sure I will get high marks; my father has seen to that! The great room is full of students. It feels good to be here, in a real school. I wish I did not have to go to the HBS, though. I would rather go to the ULO, the vocational school where I could study theater and dance, but that is not good enough for one of Pap's children.

The clock on the wall shows it is time—nine o'clock, and sure enough, the proctors begin to file in, just as Pap said they would. They are dressed in suits and ties and they look very serious. This is a serious occasion. Pap said to expect a surprise. I wonder if I will get a gift when I get home.

I examine each proctor. These will be my HBS instructors, Pap says. Then, through the door, comes my surprise: Pap. My jaw drops open in horror. Pap is moving up to the HBS? I am not through with him as a teacher? I manage to get my mouth shut and the shock off my face by the time his eyes find me, and he smiles.

I am still in prison, every afternoon and most evenings. Whenever I ask Pap if I can go to a party or a dance with my friends from the HBS, he is suspicious that I have a boyfriend. "You want to play around?" he says. "You play around with your books—there they are." And I am left alone with my studies. I hate Math and Science, the subjects that are taught by Pap.

My friends at school think I am so lucky. "He is your father! You will get high marks!" They have no idea. I have twice as much homework as they, and if I make a mistake on a test, I must keep taking new tests until I get everything right. He makes me get up in front of the class, and he ridicules me when I cannot explain the question he has put to me. But this is the way things are, and I have to accept it. I have no choice.

I know Bolle feels sorry for me. I cry every morning; it is all I can do to get myself out the door to go to school. It is like a sadness that drags me down, down, down, and I am so heavy I cannot move or think beyond the heaviness. So far I have been able to overcome the heaviness, but this morning, I cannot stop crying, and I cannot get out of bed.

"Ilse, you will be late if you do not get up now," Bolle tells me. I hear her voice, but I am too tired to respond, and I close my eyes.

Maybe minutes, maybe hours or days later—I don't know because I am drifting in a sleep world—I am aware of my step-mother standing beside my bed. My father stands behind her.

"Come, my girl, your mother will help you dress. We are going to see the doctor."

It turns out I have had a "breakdown." I have too much stress. Pap and the doctor blame it on the high expectations of the HBS—too much for a girl who missed four years of schooling and must struggle to keep up. Bosh! I could keep up with the expectations of the HBS just fine. It is my father's expectations that have put me in this condition.

The cure, the doctor says, is to give me time to rest, and then I am to go to the *Meer Uitgebreid Lager Onderwijs,* the MULO that Bolle attends. I would still prefer the ULO which would prepare me to go to work, but I am glad to be rid of the HBS and Pap's bullying, and I will welcome Bolle's company. In the meantime, I will enjoy the rest. I will enjoy my brothers and sisters who bring me presents and visit with me. I will enjoy the good food the kokki brings to me. I am grateful that I am safe and clean and that Pap is being kind. I love to play with Caddy and little Judy and, for the moment, my stepmother is being friendly. I will still not call her "Mam," and I do not want anything to do with her son, Fred. I will never forget the beating I took, I am sure, on his behalf.

Pap is talking to Fred in the office. Talking is not the best word for it—it sounds more like another battle, but this time I am not one of the combatants. It turns out that Fred has been mishandling the books of the Netherlands-Indies Education Association. One thing my father cannot tolerate is humiliation, and he has been dealt a huge dose of it. Fred has been marking members "Unpaid" and pocketing their dues. We can hear it all from the dining room, Bolle, my stepmother, and I. Bolle clings to her mother who clenches her teeth and breathes hard and glares at me. I try to keep the smile off my face, but I am not very successful.

"They had receipts, Fred. They had receipts to show me."

"Well I don't know how they got receipts, Pap."

"They are in your handwriting. Signed by you."

"They must have forged them. Haven't you ever heard of forgery?"

Fred is a sassy one. I am surprised Pap has not landed the first blow yet.

"Fred, you are a liar, and you are a thief." Pap has it right, at last. He should have listened to me a long time ago and he would have saved himself the embarrassment of going to his Association meeting and accusing colleagues of failing to pay their dues.

"Get out of my sight," Pap bellows. What? Fred is not going to get a beating? I cannot hide my disappointment. "Tell your mother I want to see her immediately."

My stepmother does not wait for Fred to tell her anything. She storms into the office as Fred storms out the front door.

"How do you dare to treat my son this way?" A new battle begins. They shout, she cries, their voices get quiet, then the volume rises and they are shouting again. There is a loud crash—I think one of them has thrown something. The little children come into the dining room, one by one, and when little Caddy starts to cry with fright, Bolle and I herd them out to the back yard. We can still hear the row going on, but not the words that are said.

Pap and his wife finally quiet down, but they are in the office for a very long time. When the kokki calls us for dinner, Bolle, Ditte and I are the adults at the table. Finally the office door opens, but my father leaves the house and his wife goes to her room. Ditte, Bolle, and I take care of the younger children and put them to bed. Everyone has cried, at one point or another. Except me.

That was the turning point of our war. It was over, but I didn't know it quite yet. Our household turned silent and we tiptoed around each other, waiting to see what would happen next. From the angry words we had heard pouring from the office that day, I knew a chasm of distrust had opened up between my father and his wife. He had confronted her with her sly mistreatment of René, Edith, Marijke, and me. He had blamed her for provoking his attack on me over the missing money.

I was vindicated. Pap knew he had been wrong. He never apologized, but he did buy me an expensive book.

Chapter 35.
Love at First Reflection

In May of 1950 Pap, René, Marijke, Edith and I boarded the S.S. Asturias, a sturdy Belfast-built ocean liner, and we set out for the Netherlands. We would learn, en route, that Pap and Noes were divorcing, but that was not the entire reason we left.

It was a choice forced upon us by the political circumstances of our beloved homeland. The Dutch East Indies had morphed into the New Republic of Indonesia. It was only a matter of time before we would be required to adopt Indonesian citizenship or take our Dutch passports and leave. Pap chose the Netherlands. He always did present himself as more Dutch than anyone else.

There was a reason for that. His father was Johan Heijneman Ferdinand Beer, a staunch Dutchman who went to Java to increase his fortune. He was smitten by Saniten, a Javanese woman, descendant of a Djokja princess we are told, and they produced four children. Pap—Hendrik—was the third in that lineup. But Pap was thirteenth in a line of fourteen children born to Johan Beer, out of five relationships, and Pap's last name was not "Beer" because Saniten and Johan were not married. Johan was already married to Margaretha. When Saniten agreed to be baptized into the Christian faith, Johan gave her the name of Johanna Evelijn Veere, and her children became Evelijn Veeres. In 1910 Johan and Margaretha divorced, and three months later

Johan married his beloved Johanna/Saniten. Shortly thereafter, little Hendrik was packed off to the Netherlands to become a Dutchman, and he didn't return until he had finished his education at the university in Amsterdam. With highest honors, of course.

I can only guess how that must have felt, leaving everything he knew and loved to go live in a boarding school in a country so different from his own. Perhaps that was when he learned to keep his own counsel, for he never talked about it. He did not have a close relationship with his parents. I always sensed he resented his banishment. I also sensed he resented his mother for being Javanese, royalty notwithstanding.

Technically we were not emigrating, we were repatriating, but the new Indonesian government allowed each of us to take only one suitcase: clothing and toiletries, nothing else. So for the second time in his forty-seven years, Pap lost his life's savings and everything he owned. We set out of that house on Gelria Straat to board the ship in Batavia carrying one suitcase each and the equivalent of $50 apiece. I was seventeen, Marijke was thirteen, René was eleven, and Edith was seven years old.

Batavia is not at all as I remember. It is hot, sticky, too many people. It does not even have the same name. Now it is Jakarta. But it is still the capital, and I suppose if we get away from this hotel we will find more of the city I remember, the one I visited with Oom Bert and Tante Zus. For three days we have been crammed into two tiny rooms in a hotel that is bursting its seams. Marijke, Edith, and I all sleep on one mattress at night, enclosed by the *klambu* which gives me claustrophobia and prevents the free circulation of much-needed air. I have never slept under mosquito netting before. I guess the mosquitoes in Jakarta carry more danger than the mosquitoes anywhere else. But given the heat, the klambu, and my two sisters flailing their arms and legs all night, I am exhausted and in none too happy a mood. Pap promises a surprise, however, for our last day, and we are waiting for him in the crowded foyer. He told us to dress well.

The couches and roomy wing-backed chairs are all taken. This would be a nice hotel if it weren't for the throngs of people stuffed into it. We are gathered around a marble pillar, Marijke, Edith, René and I. I lean against the pillar to absorb some of its coolness, and I hear Pap's voice.

"Ah, I have spied them," he says.

He is with a tiny white-haired lady who carries a white cane over her arm. Pap's arm is around her shoulders, protecting her from the crush of people, his other arm at her elbow, guiding her. She shuffles along as Pap leads her to stand in front of me.

"Here we are," he says, and he takes his hand away from her elbow.

Her hand reaches out, groping, until it finds me. Then both hands cover my face with light little flickering touches, and her face lights up in smile lines.

"Ilse! It is Ilse, am I right?"

"Oma!" I gasp. It is my Oma Evelijn Veere! "Oh yes, you are right! I am Ilse." And I am suddenly in the embrace of my father's mother. René was a babe in Mam's arms the last time I saw her—eleven years ago? Could it be so long? And Edith had not been heard of.

One by one, she "sees" each of the others with her flickering fingertips. It is a strange experience, to be seen in such a way, but nice when it is your own grandmother and when she is so sweet and kind. I recognize Pap and Tante Annie in her face. Square jaw, dimpled chin even among the wrinkles, high cheekbones and beautiful arched eyebrows. Even though she is blind, she has warm brown eyes, and even though she must have an inclination to lean forward to meet the unexpected in her blindness, she stands very straight. In that, I am like her, although in most other ways I resemble my mother.

Pap takes us to an eating place where we can sit down. I wonder where my grandfather is, but I don't ask. He may be dead, and I would be embarrassed to admit I do not know. Or my father may not want to see him, and that would be embarrassing, too. Now that we have settled into conversation, the whirlwind of surprise and excitement over, I realize she has come to say goodbye, and this goodbye is forever. My chest tightens, and I fight to keep from spoiling this happy time with tears.

My sense of the final goodbye is still with me on the fantail of the Asturias. It is a wonder the ship doesn't tip backwards, nose up in the air, with so many of us out on deck, catching our last glimpse of Java. I am looking at the last spot of green in the Emerald Girdle, a mere dot in the blue of the ocean. Then it is gone. Farewell Indies. You now belong to someone else. The orchids will bloom, but I will not be there to see them. I will never forget you.

The anticipation of our new future wins out over the sorrow of leaving my home and leaving the old ones. Best of all, since we drove away from the house on Gelria Straat Pap has become so *menselijk,* so human. He is not professor or taskmaster, determined to make his daughter into something she is not—a scholar. He is not judge or jury, responsible for keeping the peace within a contentious home. He is just Pap, comfortable with his children and fun to be with. I might be able to talk with him, now, about those years we were apart, but I won't. I don't want to run the risk of spoiling this happiness by bringing up unhappiness that has passed. I don't want him to shoot darts at me with his eyes and say "We will not speak of that nonsense!" I do not want my painful memories of Mam to come between us.

So we all give ourselves over to the pleasure of the voyage with only the view of the white ocean beyond the ship's rails. Every day it is smooth, like a mirror. My Bandung friends' warnings of pitching and rolling and seasickness prove false. The food on board is delicious, and it all stays put!

We are lined up on deck, looking forward to the first glimpse of Holland and the dunes. Just as I watched my old life fade into the horizon, I now watch my new life come into view. As the Asturias approaches Hoek van Holland—the hook—we see green lawns and Dutch houses with dormers and pointed gables. At last, in the North Sea Canal, we will soon be entering the great harbor of Amsterdam. The last twenty-eight days have been the happiest of my life, certainly since the Japanese came into it eight years ago. Oh, if Mam could only have been a part of it. But she has been with us. In my heart.

Ocean liners, I learn, do not just pull up to a dock and let everyone get off. It takes forever to maneuver through the locks, then through the busy canals, and finally to our assigned berth. Pap takes charge and directs us into the passenger terminal and through the customs and immigration line. I am glad it is June and we will not have to deal with snow and ice quite yet. Most of my clothes will be appropriate through the summer season.

At last, we climb into a taxi and Pap gives the driver the address of the pension which will be our new home: Nieuwe Keizers Gracht 18. I watch very carefully as we make our way out of the port complex and into the city, through narrow streets with tall buildings rising on both sides, hiding the sky. I squeeze my elbows to my sides, as I feel I am in danger of being crushed. Am I in prison, again? And the noise! Clang, clang, clang, beep beep—streetcars and busses sound their presence. Ding, ding—bicycle bells, hundreds and hundreds of bicycles everywhere I look. The sidewalks are jammed with people walking fast, as if they are all late for an appointment. I have never seen this before. This is my home now. Will I ever get used to it?

We turn onto a street that borders a canal. Whew, the sky opens up again, at least on one side, and it is much quieter. My elbows relax. Along the canal side of the street are parked a few cars and fleets of bicycles. On the other side stand two-, three-, and four-storied houses. They are all connected in a row and they are all brick, but each is unique—some dark brown, some red, some yellow, some sand-colored. Some are wide, some narrow, some tall, some squat. Some have tall narrow windows, some have arched windows, some have wide "picture" windows, and the windows from house to house do not line up. All of the houses have light colored trim of different widths and designs, as if each is trying to be as different as possible from its neighbors. Each building is topped by a gable that is shaped unlike any other, and under the gable, big double windows— more like doors—that appear to open. Sticking out of an attic space above these high doors, many have a large hook that looks like it moves up and down on a chain. Curious. I will have to learn about such things.

Trees grow up out of holes in the concrete along the canal, and bushes and flowers grow out of pots and flower boxes in front of the houses. The taxi pulls up in front of one that is tall and narrow with a wide stoop that stretches across two buildings and has a flight of stairs at either end. People going into #18 use the stairs at the left. Those going into #17 use the stairs at the right. An iron railing divides the stoop, right down the middle. On the ground floor, below the stoop, are windows with curtains and flowers on the sills, and a door. Someone lives there, too, looking at eye-level onto the wide sidewalk.

This is our pension, the boarding house that will be our home. Pap pays the driver, we collect our bags, and we line up behind Pap who leads us up the stairs to the front door and rings the bell marked "Office." The lady who answers is the owner of the building, and it turns out she lives on the ground floor—under the stoop. She invites us into a spacious front hall with marble floors. An elegant stairway with a gleaming, molded wooden banister rises upward, turning a corner at each floor. It is dizzying to look up through the middle and see the ceiling four stories up. Our landlady is friendly enough and asks about our voyage as we climb two flights of the stairs. When she unlocks our door, we break rank and pour into the apartment—two rooms, light and airy, with high ceilings, tall windows, and furnishings, of course. We bring nothing to our new home but our clothes, and precious few of them.

When the landlady says, "Dinner is at 6 o'clock," I notice our rooms do not include a kitchen. There is, however, a large round dining table—oak, I think—in the room that looks out over the canal, the front room. Six matching chairs circle the table. One more than we need. Then I notice a short counter with a small sink and an open dish cupboard that runs along one wall.

"We eat in our own quarters," says the landlady. "Mattheuw will deliver your tray."

She hands the key to Pap and leaves us alone to get acquainted with our new home. It is a warm afternoon—we will have no need, until autumn, of the great brick fireplace cut into the wall on one side of the room. I raise the wide window that opens over the street. We can lean over the deep sill. Marijke and I inspect a mirror that is attached to a swivel arm that hangs out from the building. It magnifies the size of the images it reflects. We swivel it toward us and make larger-than-life faces at each other in the mirror.

"No, no," Pap says, leaning over the sill. "This is what you do." He trains the mirror on the sidewalk below, onto the front door of the building.

"Now we can see who is ringing our bell," he explains. "If it is someone to whom we owe money, we are not at home!"

We all laugh. What a clever idea, the magnifying reflecting mirror. I hope Pap is joking about not being home to debtors, as I hope we have no debtors.

We choose our rooms—girls in the big front room, René and Pap in the smaller back room. The beds are in the walls, behind curtains, and when we are ready for bed, we pull them down and voilá, our beds are ready to sleep in. But first we must make them up with the bedding we find stacked on chairs in each of the rooms. And we have different ideas of where the furniture should be placed. We are in the midst of rearranging our new home when we hear a knock at the door. It is six o'clock—dinnertime!

Pap rolls down his sleeves and reaches for his suit jacket. He nods to me and I open the door. He steps forward to greet Mattheuw. But no one is there. Pap and I look at each other, and then we look down. There is the tray full of food.

"Hmph," says Pap. "I must pick up my dinner from the floor?" I can see he considers this unacceptable.

Marijke and I hurry to set the table with the dishes and utensils we find in the cupboard. We remove the domed covers from the dishes. Roast something, sliced and swimming in a gravy of some kind; something white that is not rice—potato purée, perhaps—plopped into a round bowl; carrots that have been sliced lengthwise and have something green sprinkled on them, and—joy of joys—tomatoes that have been sliced into thick, juicy slabs. My brother and my sisters and I dish up, and I am concentrating on the tomato slab.

Pap samples the fluffy white stuff and confirms it is potato purée. "Baby food!" he says. He pushes the meat around on his plate, taking a taste of the brown sauce that covers it.

"Slop!" he says. "Come on, we are going to find something to eat that is fit for human consumption!"

I think this food is fit, and I can tell my brother and sisters would like to stay and eat it, too, but we all get up from the table and follow Pap down the stairs and out the door. Many of the buildings house businesses—some of them restaurants—on the sidewalk level. We walk down the street until we find one that says "Indian Cuisine."

"That is close enough," Pap announces, and we go in to spend some of our meager funds on our first full meal in Amsterdam.

A few days after our arrival, the weather is beautiful and Pap returns from a stroll along the canal. "Come," he announces. "It is time to go shopping for more appropriate clothing."

It takes me back to the shopping spree in Batavia when Oom Bert treated us to new wardrobes—beautiful, colorful clothes.

But the spree takes a downward spin at the first boutique when Pap makes it clear that colorful clothes are not for us.

"It calls too much attention to your dark skin," he explains.

I never worried about anyone paying attention to the color of my skin before, and I wonder why it is an issue now. We pass over very attractive items and end up with dark greens and browns and navy blues. It isn't even July yet, but my father insists we all buy coats for the winter. I guess he wants to be prepared. The coat my father chooses for me is hideous. It is a long, shapeless thing made of wool, and it must weigh ten pounds. Worse yet, it is dark, dark, mud brown. I hate it, but at least I can stuff it away in the closet until the weather turns cold. Maybe moths will find it. I would be happy to draw them a map.

One of my favorite pastimes is to sit at the open window and watch the activities on the *gracht*, the canal. Tourist boats keep our gracht busy. "Toot, toot," they pipe when they approach a bridge, to make sure a boat approaching from the other direction stays on its own side. In summer, the ear is never very far away from the sound of boat horns. I like to make up stories about the people I see from our window—little dramatic vignettes that keep me entertained. Directly across the canal from our window is an old folks' home. I see them, stooped and lame, some in wheelchairs, and I wonder where they were, what they did when they were my age. I peer down at the houseboats lodged against the concrete wall on our side of the canal, and I wonder what it would be like to live in a house that rises and falls with the lapping water. Pleasant, I think, remembering our passage on the Asturias.

One day, as autumn begins to give in to winter and I must put on my wool sweater to take my place at the open window,

I spy a young man in the reflecting mirror. My breath catches, I blink, and my heart does a flippety-flop in my chest. I watch for the brief moment it takes him to stroll out of range. On an impulse, I adjust the mirror and watch him just a little longer. He is very handsome, and he walks gracefully, with confidence. I blush at my own audacity for admiring the way a strange man walks, and I hurry to train the mirror again on the front door. It is very near dinnertime, so I go in to set the table, just in case the dinner is suitable tonight and we get to eat at home. Pap has not gotten any more tolerant of mashed potatoes and gravy.

It becomes a habit to watch the reflecting mirror in the minutes before dinner, to catch a glimpse of the handsome young man. I even imagine that he lingers a bit as he passes by the front door, and sometimes he stops and looks up. His eyes seem to be searching, but I step back so I am safely hidden from his view. I would be mortified to be caught looking at him, even though it has become the high point of my day. Pap has made social connections since our arrival, and he brings young Indies home for me to meet. But none of them measure up to the dark-haired, fair-skinned Dutchman in the mirror. I am crazy. He doesn't know I exist, and yet I make myself cry with beautiful made-up stories about him.

Winter sets in and I must put on my ugly brown coat before I open the window. I am grateful for its warmth, for I now have a new diversion—watching the skaters on the canal. They must stay out in the middle to avoid being a nuisance to the residents of the houseboats, locked in for the winter by the thick ice. I lean over the sill to get as close to the skaters as I can. Oh, they go so fast, and if they are skating for pleasure, they perform such graceful movements, like dancing. I can't get enough of watching them, and then one day I see him. His shiny black hair is covered by a white knitted cap, striped in brown. He is the most graceful skater of them all, and I can't take my eyes off him. Marijke comes to the window.

"Ilse," she says, "I think the one with the white and brown hat is looking this way."

"Nonsense!" I say, but I think so too. My eyes are riveted on him; I cannot look away.

He disappears out of sight, and then here he comes, streaking down the canal faster than I have ever seen anyone skate. Is he showing off for me, or is my imagination working as fast as those skates? He looks toward our open window, straight at me, when a toddler just learning to skate wobbles into his path. I throw up my hands and scream. He looks down in time to scoop up the little one and skate down-canal with the child in his arms. I burst into tears with the nearness of such a disaster, and by the time he returns the bawling toddler to its mother, I am watching from my chair inside, shaken to the core. Oh, but he was so heroic.

The next day, earlier than usual, I am at the window making up yet another story around my young Dutch hero. I reach out and play with the mirror, turning it slowly, this way and that, up and down, and then I cannot believe my eyes. In the mirror, perfectly centered, is the face of my handsome Dutchman. He is smiling directly into my eyes, and my heart leaps its boundaries. As soon as I can breathe again, I lean out the window to look for him. He is leaning out the third-story window of the house two doors away— Nieuwe Keizers Gracht 20. He looks down at me, and we wave to each other.

I cannot stop smiling.

Epilogue

Everything that happened to me, to our family, from the outset of the Japanese occupation to the forced repatriation, led me to Jan (pronounced the Dutch way—"Yawn"), the man in the mirror. He became a regular visitor. Poor Pap continued to bring home educated Indies lads, but I loved the handsome Dutchman who lived two houses away and created artistic lamps for the family business at Nieuwe Keizers Gracht 20.

Jan led me forward into a new life I could never have imagined in my most creative stories. I turned out to be wrong about having only one mam; Jan's parents drew me into their family, and I thought of them as Mam and Pap Smit long before I had the right to call them that. Jan and I were married in 1954, and we moved into the Smits' top story—three flights up! Jan had spent our engagement period transforming the attic storage area into an adorable apartment that was the envy of all my friends.

Pap was not altogether approving of our marriage, but little Erik changed that. Pap became a doting Opa. Erik put dents in his Opa's armor of reserve, but never enough to enable Pap to tell his story, listen to mine, or say he was sorry—about anything. Oh, poor Pap, he was such a victim of his own silence. And he was lonely.

Just as he had brought Indies boys home for me to inspect, I offered him respectable ladies of appropriate age and disposition. But he wanted Noes back, and he wanted his children, Caddy and Judy—my young half-brother and half-sister. Since his pride would not allow him to ask Noes to come to Holland, he gave the job to me, but he dictated every word. "I fear for his health," I wrote as my father directed. It worked. She left Indonesia, and they remarried in Amsterdam.

In 1957 Jan and I left our families and emigrated to the United States, carrying with us two of Pap's paintings. "To remember me by," Pap said when he gave them to me. I treasure them. He died in 1959 with his story still locked inside. His wife died much later. I was glad Pap had companionship in his final years, but I never obeyed the mandate to call the woman "Mam."

Imagine our surprise when Jan, Erik, and I ended up in Seattle. We thought our destination was Washington, the nation's capital! Two little brothers—Fritz and Jeff—and one little sister—Monique—joined Erik as the years went by. Life was good until the day a drunk driver slammed into our Fritz on the street outside our house. He was fifteen years old. As a child, I lost my mother; as a mother, I lost my child. As a family we helped each other move on, but my beautiful boy is never far from me, in my memory.

What a man, Jan. When I formed an Indonesian dance troupe, he became my set designer, photographer, sound technician, avid fan, and costume assistant. My costumes won a national trophy. I think my childhood butterfly designs found their way into those costumes. When I started a little business to sell exotic Indonesian spices and Dutch delicacies he created a wonderful shop and we added a cubbyhole coffee shop for our customers. When I decided to expand the shop into a full-fledged Indonesian restaurant, he turned it into a piece of the Emerald Girdle and we called it Restaurant Bali.

When we retired from our many labors, we chose an island—Whidbey Island, near Seattle—and Jan turned our seven acres into a showcase of gardens and lawns. Little by little, livestock began to gather until we had twenty-four hens, two roosters, seven sheep, three goats, one dog, and a family of ducks that had their own pond with a Jan-built island in the middle of it. Most of the animals treated me with indifference, but they all vied for Jan's attention. I could not turn my back on the billy goat, as he would butt me out of the way at every opportunity. And I'll never forget the day a cheeky rooster tippy-toed up and grabbed a lighted cigarette from Jan's hand. Off he ran with the cigarette hanging from his beak, puffing smoke in his wake. Jan could never stop laughing over that one. "If only I'd had a movie camera," he said.

One day in 1998, out on the front deck of our home, Jan fell backward without a word or a sound, and he was gone. My beloved Jan. He is with me every second of every minute of every day. He protected me from the deep sadness and the fear that sometimes overtook me, and his memory protects me still. But even Jan could not fully lift the burden imposed by silence.

So many young survivors of the camps and the Bersiap period were discouraged from relating their accounts. Parents, like Pap, refused to talk or listen. Family and strangers alike urged us to forget the past and to carry on with the present.

"Do not bother anyone with your troubles."

"If you remember, keep your memories to yourself."

"We are Hollanders now. Why do you want to bring up the ugly past?"

Long and painful silence has predicable consequences. There is no outlet for the traumatic memories except in nightmares that can happen day or night. There is no sense of belonging, only of being alone—an aloneness not understood even by spouses or children. You see, as long as I am unable to share my story, I alone carry its burden.

But enough about me.

Tante Zus adopted the sickly child, left Batavia, and spent most of her life in Holland. She never learned what became of Oom Ruud. At the end of her life, a bitter and broken woman, she pooled her resources and her strength and flew to find refuge with friends in California. But her failing health betrayed her, and she collapsed in flight. René, with his kindhearted wife, willingly cared for her in their San Diego home. But she called for me, over and over. Finally René arranged for our aunt to fly to Seattle. Again Zus collapsed on the airplane and was met on arrival by an ambulance that took her to the hospital where she lay comatose for days. I never left her side.

Late one night Tante Zus's eyes opened wide with delight as she recognized me.

"Come close," she whispered, and I stepped up to gather her frail body into my arms. She died in my embrace.

Oom Bert Fiedeldij continued his service with the Dutch Indies military until the Republican Army of the new Republic of Indonesia prevailed. In 1950 he rejoined his family in Australia and they, too, moved to the Netherlands. His daughter, Stella, who shared her father's love of flying, became a licensed pilot in her teens. A few years later she was killed when her plane crashed. Oom Bert never fully recovered from his grief.

We finally learned that Tante Annie and Oom Theo had been on their way to New Guinea when they said goodbye amidst the chaos at Hotel Ambarawa. Life was difficult for them at first, but they were able, after five long years, to send for their children and resume their life as a family in New Guinea.

And my siblings, whose lives are so interwoven with mine in this story? René emigrated to the United States as a student. He is a successful engineer in Southern California. Marijke married the son of Pap's college chum, and they raised five children. They live in Holland. Edith, who also lives in Holland, raised two children and is a talented artist who loves the outdoors. She hikes, backpacks and travels to exotic places.

All of them—René, Marijke, and Edith, along with my children—plotted a surprise visit to celebrate my 75th birthday. I hated to let them know that I found out ahead of time, that their surprise had fizzled. But the final surprise was on me. As we hugged and kissed and cried in joy to see each other, a lovely, tall, auburn-haired woman stood outside the circle. Finally I turned to her, in confusion.

"Do you not know your own sister?" she asked in Dutch, and she held her arms wide. I hugged my half-sister, Judy, for the first time in fifty-one years.

For the next two weeks, we all talked. We shared stories and feelings that had been buried for over a half a century. At last, within our own family, we began to end the silence.

In telling my story I not only end my silence, I call for others to tell their stories. Historical memory fades, but I want our eyewitness accounts to enlighten future generations as to what happened and what can happen. My story offers a means for healing in an imperfect world. Perhaps now I can lay down my burden and rest.

Guide to People and Places

People

Johan Heijneman Ferdinand Beer (*Joh-hahn* **Hay**-nuh-muhn *Bair*) – Ilse's Dutch grandfather, her father's father.

Ditte Brueur (*Dee-tuh* **Brew**-er) – Older daughter of Noes Brueur; Ilse's stepsister.

Fred Brueur (**Brew**-er) – Older son of Noes Brueur; Ilse's stepbrother.

Irma Brueur (**Brew**-er), "Bolle" (**Boh**-luh) – Younger caughter of Noes Brueur; Ilse's stepsister.

Robby Brueur (**Brew**-er) – Younger son of Noes Brueur; Ilse's stepbrother.

Rosalie Josephine Brueur (**Brew**-er), "Noes" (*Nooss*) – Second wife of Hendrik Evelijn Veere; Ilse's stepmother.

Oom Ruud Doyer (*Rood Dwah-***yay**) – Ilse's uncle, Tante Zus's husband.

Tante Zus Doyer (**Tahn**-tuh *Zooss Dwah-***yay**) – Ilse's aunt, her mother's younger sister.

Edith Evelijn Veere (**Ay**-duth *Eh-vuh-***layn**-veer) – Ilse's youngest sister, born in Surabaya, 1943.

Erik Evelijn Veere (*Erik Eh-vuh-***layn**-veer) – Ilse's older brother, born in 1929, died in1933 when Ilse was a baby.

Hendrik Evelijn Veere (**Hen**-drik *Eh-vuh-***layn**-veer), "Henk"– Ilse's father, born in Tejal, Java in 1903, son of Indiesa mother and Dutch father.

Ilse Evelijn Veere *(Il-suh Eh-vuh-layn-veere)* – The story's narrator, born in Bandung, Java in 1933.

Johanna Evelijn Veere *(Yoh-Hah-nuh Eh-vuh-layn Veer)* – Ilse's Javanese grandmother, her father's mother.

Maria Christina Elizabeth Evelijn Veere *(Maria Christina Eh-vuh-layn-veer)* "Mies" *(Meess)*– Ilse's mother, born in Modjokerto, Java in1904, daughter of Indiesa mother and Dutch father.

Marijke Evelijn Veere *(Mah-ray-kuh Eh-vuh-layn-veer)* "Mieke" *(Mee-kuh)*– Ilse's younger sister, born in Bandung, 1937.

René Evelijn Veere *(Ruh-Nay Eh-vuh-layn-veer)* – Ilse's younger brother, born in Medan, 1939.

Oom Bert Fieddeldij *(Oom Bairrt Fee-duhl-day)* – Ilse's uncle, her mother's older brother, a high ranking officer in the Royal Dutch East Indies Air Force.

Oma Fieddeldij *(Oh-mah Fee-duhl-day)* – Ilse's Indiesa grandmother, her mother's mother.

Opa Fieddeldij *(OH-pah Fee-duhl-day)* – Ilse's Dutch grandfather, her mother's father.

Tante Annie Gerrits *(Tahn-tuh Ah-nee Gair-its)* – Ilse's aunt, her father's sister, who lived in Oro-oro Ombo in the Soember Brantas.

Oom Theo Gerrits *(Oom Tay-oh Gair-its)* – Ilse's uncle who ran a coffee plantation in the Soember Brantas, Tante Annie's husband.

Gurkhas *(Gur-kuhs)* – Turbaned soldiers from Nepal who served in the British army; helped to restore order in the Dutch East Indies after the Japanese capitulated in1945.

Hasegawa *(Ha-suh-ga-wuh)* –Commander of Camp Halmaheira.

Henk – Nickname for "Hendrik," Ilse's father.

Martukosumo *(Mahr-too-kuh-soo-moh)* – A leader of the permudas in Oro-oro Ombo.

Mieke *(Mee-kuh)* – Nickname for Marijke, Ilse's sister.

Mientje *(Meen-chuh)* – Affectionate (diminutive) name for Ilse's younger cousin, Mien, daughter of Tante Annie and Oom Theo.

Mies *(Meess)* - Nickname for "Maria," Ilse's mother.

Saniten – *(Sahn-uh-tuhn)* – Ilse's grandmother's Javanese name, before she was baptized Johanna Evelijn Veere.

Jan Smit *(Yahn Smit)* – Ilse's Dutch husband, born in Bloemendaal, Holland in 1929.

Sukarno *(Soo-kahr-no)* – Leader of the revolution which resulted in an independent Indonesia in 1950. Became the first president of the Republic of Indonesia.

Takahase *(Tah-kuh-hah-see)* – Kempetai officer at Camp Halmaheira.

Captain Raymond Westerling – The commander of a special Dutch army commando unit that fought against the Indonesians' bid for independence; he was notorious for his murderous treatment of insurgents and their suspected collaborators.

Places

Ambarawa (Ahm-bahr-**ah**-wuh) – A city in Central Java, where Fort Willem II was located.

Bali *(Bah-lee)* – Island across the narrow Bali Strait from Surabaya, East Java.

Bandung *(Bahn-doong)* – City in West Java; Ilse's birthplace.

Batavia *(Buh-tah-vee-uh)* – City in West Java, capitol of the Dutch East Indies; later re-named Jakarta.

Brantas River *(**Brahn**-tuss River)* – A river which originates in the mountainous region of East Java.

Camp Halmaheira *(Camp Hahl-muh-**hair**-uh)* – A Japanese concentration camp for women and children, run by the Kempeitai military police in Semarang, Central Java.

Cikapundung River *(See-kuh-**poon**-doong River)* – A river in Bandung.

De Hotel *(Duh Hotel)* - A large hotel in Surabaya that housed displaced Dutch citizens during the Japanese occupation. (Actual name unkown.)

Dutch East Indies – A Dutch colony from 1797 to 1949; the archipelago was renamed Indonesia after WWII when it gained independence from the Netherlands.

Emerald Girdle – A poetic term for the Dutch East Indies, as the archipelago "drapes" around the equator like an "emerald girdle."

Fort Willem II – A historical penitentiary in Central Java which became a center for Dutch and Indies refugees after the Japanese capitulated in 1945.

Gelria Straat *(Hhel-**ree**-uh straht)* – The street, in Bandung, where the blended family of Noes Brueur and Henk Evelijn Veere moved after Henk's children reunited with their father.

Indonesia – The name given to the new nation in 1950 after the revolutionaries gained independence from the Netherlands.

Java *(**Jah**-vuh)* – The most heavily populated island of the Dutch East Indies, where the capitol of the unified nation of Indonesia is located.

Jakarta *(Juh-**kar**-tuh)* – The capitol of Indonesia, located in West Java; once Batavia, the city was renamed Jakarta after Indonesia gained independence from the Netherlands.

Kalianget *(Kah-lee-ah-nuht)* – Town on the southern shore of the island of Madura, famed for its white sands.

Madura (Mah-**doo**-ruh) - A small island where Ilse's family once lived, located off the northeastern coast of Java.

Medan *(May-duhn)* – A city where Ilse's family once lived, on the northeastern coast of the island of Sumatra which is located north of Java.

Oro-oro Ombo *Or-oh-or-oh **Ohm**-boh)* – A rural town in the Soember Brantas in East Java, near the plantation of Oom Theo, Ilse's uncle.

Semarang *(Suh-**mah**-rong)* – The city on the northern coast of Central Java where Camp Halmaheira was located.

Soember Brantas *(**Soom**-bair **Brahn**-tuhs)* – A mountainous region in East Java, where the Brantas River originates.

Sumatra *(Soo-**mah**-truh)* – An island north of Java, largest of the fully Indonesian islands.

Surabaya *(Soo-ruh-**by**-uh)* – City on the northern coast of East Java, where Ilse's family moved just prior to the Japanese occupation in 1942.

Tjakranagara Weg *(Juh-**krah**-nuh-**gah**-ruh Way)* – The street in Bandung where Ilse's father lived and where he was reunited with his children after WWII.

Glossary of Foreign Words and Phrases

Key: D – Dutch

M – Maleis (bahasa, the standard Indonesian language or passar, the informal native language)

J – Japanese

alang-alang – M, Tall, sharp-bladed native grass, thick at the base.

anak – M, Child, polite address to use when speaking to a child.

anglo – M, Small terra cotta clay cooking stove, fueled by wood or charcoal.

babu – M, Female; polite address to use when speaking to a woman.

babu kokki – M, Female cook, polite address.

bahasa – M, Language.

Bahasa Maleis – M, Standard language of the Dutch East Indies; also called Malay. Now called Bahasa Indonesia.

bakkar – **M**, Method of grilling directly over hot coals.

bali bali – M, Small, cot-sized bed, with a mattress.

bambu runtjing – M, Deadly poison, used on spear tips.

bedjak – M, Three-wheeled pedaled taxi.

berang – M, Spicy eggplant dish.

beras – M, Rice.

bikkelen – D, Game played with small metal manipulatives called *bikkele,* and a smallrubber ball.

bitter bollen – D, Small, spicy meatballs, rolled in fine bread crumbs and deep fried.

blimbing – M, Starfruit that grows wild in the tropics.

brandgang – D, Alley space that acts as a firebreak between walled compounds.

botol cebok – M, Process of cleaning oneself after bathrooming.

buah klappa quadrat – M, Baked coconut pudding, cut into squares for serving.

bubur dedek – M, Brown rice porridge, or gruel, with husks mixed in.

daon pandan – M, A green leaf with a distinctive flavor, used as a spice.

dase – J, Give it to me!

désa – M, Native village in a rural area.

dinkliek – M, Low stool, used for sitting.

discus werpeh - D, The sport of discus throwing.

djongos – M, Butler.

dokar – M, Horse-drawn cart used as a public conveyance.

doorgang – D, Half-way house; transitional quarters.

farspringen - D, Broad jump.

fijver – D, Pond.

flamboya – D, Broadleaf tree with bright red blossoms; spreads a wide canopy.

frikadel goreng – M, Meatballs.

gaar keuken – D, Kitchen.

gang – D, Hallway.

gedek – M, Fence made of woven bamboo.

gobang– M, Coin worth about 2 ½ cents.

gotrik – M, Game played with bat-like sticks, in which a wooden puck is scooped up from a low platform and then batted; the player who hits the puck farthest wins.

gracht – D, Canal.

grobak – M, Ox-drawn flatbed cart.

gudang – D, Store room.

gula djawa – M, Javanese palm sugar.

gunjin-san – J, Polite way of addressing a soldier.

HBS (Hogere Burger School) – D, Academic high school, university preparation.

Hollander – D, The term used for a full-blooded Dutch person.

ice lilin – M, Sweet crushed-ice treats.

Indies(male) or Indiesa (female) – D, The term used for a mixed-blood person, part Dutch.

isoge – J, Hurry up!

pjinda kaas – D, Peanut butter.

kandoke - M, Cook's assistant.

kangkung – M, Spinach-like greens seasoned with tangy spices.

kapala kongsie – M, Head of a household, supervisor, "house mother."

Kapala kongsie-wa,dokoda – J, Where is the house mother?

katjang pandjang – M, Long green beans.

katjung – M, Servant, assistant to the butler; general handy man.

keirei – J, Bow down!

Kempetai – J, Japanese special military police force, known for brutality.

kipas – M, Small fan.

klambu – M, Mosquito netting.

kleine worstje – D, Little sausages.

klepon – M, Sweet rice balls, colored green with *daon pandan,* wrapped around a thimbleful of palm sugar.

knickers – D, Game of marbles.

KNIL: Koninklijk Nederlands Indisch Leger – The Royal Netherlands East Indies Army kokki – M, Female cook.

kolak – M, Chilled coconut drink.

kondah – M, Bun of wound-up hair, pinned to the crown of the head.

koolie – M, Laborer.

krygertje – D, Game of tag.

kumpulan – M, Official gathering.

kuweeh mangkok – M, Sweet steamed muffin cakes.

laos root – M, Root used to spice Indonesian foods.

lever pastij – D, Chopped liver spread.

luier – D, Diaper.

Maleis – M, The language spoken in the Dutch East Indies, also called Malay, now called Bahasa Indonesia or simply Indonesian.

mami – D, A child's address for "mother"; mommy.

mandi bak – M, The large tiled cistern of water in the small room used for dip-bucket showers.

Miesje – D, Young girl.

menselijk – D, The quality of being humane, sympathetic, approachable.

merdeka – M, Freedom: a slogan-cry of Indonesian revolutionaries during their fight for independence.

mid-dag dutje – D, Midday nap.

MULO (Meer Uitgebreid Lager Onderwijs) – D, High school, leads to polytechnical college course.

naore – J, Stand up straight!

ojyou-san – J, Polite way of addressing a woman; miss.

oma – D, Grandmother.

omae – J, The pronoun, "you."

oom – D, Uncle.

opa – D, Grandfather.

papi – *D*, A child's address for "father"; daddy.

pasar – *M*, Open air market.

Pasar Baru – *M*, Farmers' market.

Pasar Maleis – *M*, Informal native language.

patjol – *M*, Hoe.

Perang sudah habis – *M*, The war is over.

pemuda – *M*, A young man; more specifically, an Indonesian nationalistic extremist during the revolutionary period following WWII.

piedjit – *D*, Back massage.

pisang goreng – *M*, Bananas dipped in batter and fried.

platje – *D*, Small patio.

Republican Pemuda Army – One of several names given to the revolutionary forces fighting for an independent Indonesian nation after WWII.

rijst – *D*, Rice.

rimbu – *M*, Patch of untended plantings.

Samurai (swords*)* – *J*, Ceremonial swords carried by the Kempetai as a sign of their elite standing in the Japanese military.

sapulidi – *M*, Bamboo tool used for beating dust out of rugs, mattresses, etc.

satay – *M*, Chunks of meat, skewered and cooked over a wood or charcoal fire, and seasoned with a spicy sauce.

Satu salah—semuah salah – *M*, When one is guilty, all are guilty.

schatjes – *D*, Affectionate term for children or loved ones.

shinai – *J*, Bamboo swords carried by Kempeitai noncommissioned officers.

shookoo-san – *J*, Polite way of addressing a military officer.

sisir-sirit – *M*, Small comb with very fine teeth, used to groom lice and nits out of hair.

Sore-ha nanda – J, What is that?

tante – D, Aunt.

tate – J, Get up!

tempeh – M, Soybean cakes.

tiekers – M, Large, colorful braided mats or rugs.

tjiplukan – M, A vine that grows along the banks of ponds and produces edible fruit.

tjutji – M, Laundry maid.

Toelatings Examen – D, Comprehensive test of skills taken by students who have completed elementary school; used to place students into secondary school.

treemakasi banjak – M, Thank you.

ulekan – M, Rock used as a pestle to grind spices.

ULO (Uitgebreid Lager Onderwijs) – D, Vocational high school, prepares students for work.

wafels – D, Sandwich cookies with honey filling.

waringin – M, Banyan tree.

warong – M, Concession stand; may be a cart or a small, stationary hut.

wasandjes – D, Bath mitt.

Westerlings – A Royal Netherlands Army unit under the command of Captain Westerling, known for atrocities committed against natives during the Indonesian revolution following WWII.

Acknowledgments

From Ilse:

I want to thank Dorothy from the depth of my heart for listening to my story, for the many hours she spent researching, writing, and crying with me to put my story into the written word, and for being there as a friend as I broke my silence. I thank my pastors, Jim Lindus and Jeff Gaustad for inspiring me to tell this story and helping me to end my silence. And thanks to my friend Ron McCamman for his encouragement. My brother René and my sisters, Edith and Marijke, as children, supported my will to carry on; without having them to care for, I might not have had the strength to survive. As adults, they have supported my will to tell our shared story; it has resulted in new understandings and tears that have brought us closer. My husband, Jan, was always there to bring me back from the dark places; without him, I might never have experienced the joy of life on the other side of those dark places. I thank my children who know, now, the part of their heritage that has been locked in silence: my sons, Eric, Fritz and Jeff, who filled my heart with joy and stood strong through my darker days of healing; and my daughter, Monique. I thank Monique for being at my side throughout her life, for giving me the chance to experience the mother-daughter relationship I missed with my mom, and for being my best friend.

From Dorothy:

The first thanks go to Ilse for trusting me with her story. What a privilege, to hear this long-overdue accounting from the lips and heart of this amazing woman. I echo the sentiment of one reader who said, "I just wanted to reach into the story and give some comfort to that poor little girl." I hope comfort has come with ending the silence.

Next, I must thank the many who nudged the manuscript along in its development and made it better with every nudge. I am indebted to the members of the Whidbey Writers' Group for their encouragement and laser-precision critiquing, and to Susan Jensen of that esteemed group, who gave the manuscript its first official line edit. I am grateful beyond measure to my husband, Dean, chief researcher and editor, and to son, Kelly and sister, Linda Ainsworth for their input and editing. John Hansen deserves thanks for his encouragement and expert historical perspectives, as does Yuka Zuver for rescuing my fractured Japanese language efforts. Thanks, also to Faye Casebeer who gave *End the Silence* its final scrutiny and found four more typos to be corrected.

Most first-book authors will agree that the hardest part of writing a book comes after the book is written: the selling, the producing, and the promoting. Ilse and I thank our agent, Gordon Warnock, who believed in this story and kept us believing, too. We're grateful to Amazon for putting the book in our hands, at last. Thank you, Pierr Morgan, artist extraordinaire, who really nailed the cover art. With expertise and good humor, Michael Stadler (of Stadler Studio Photography) produced our bio photos and our first filmed video, "The Handkerchief." It hit the YouTube scene, thanks to our technology mentor and ever-patient advisor, Terry, a.k.a. my darling daughter. More thanks to Tom Masters, who put us on the blogosphere in record time, and to Paul Lien who was ever-ready to help us with the photo pages. Huge thanks go to Joan Cartan-Hansen, Idaho Public Television producer, who had enough faith in us to put us on the air in her Dialogue show.

Finally, we thank Bianca Dias-Halpert for her friendship and encouragement. She is dedicated to preserving the Indo culture through The Indo Project. With Bianca's help, along with Jan Krancher, author of *The Defining Years of the Dutch East Indies,* we have communicated with Indo people around the globe. It has been a profound privilege.

About the Author

Dorothy Read is active as a writer and as a mentor of writers. She has served as the chair of the Whidbey Island Writers Association and has served on the committee that presents the annual Whidbey Island Writers Conference. Her short stories have been anthologized in four Whidbey Writers Group books (Gull Rock Publishing); two Rocking Chair Reader editions (Adams Media); *Sea of Voices, Isle of Story* (Triple Tree Publishing); and *Soundings Review*, the literary magazine of Whidbey Writers Workshop.

To contact Dorothy Read, or to purchase additional copies of *End the Silence,* visit www.dorothyread.com

Resources
To learn more about the Dutch/Indo experience during World War II and the diaspora that followed, and to connect with today's active Dutch/Indo community, visit the following websites and follow the links they offer.

The Indo Project: http://theindoproject.org/
Dutch-Indonesian Community: http://dutcheastindies.web.id/
Peter van der Kuil: http://members.iinet.net.au/~vanderkp/